Robert Richard Randall

Copy of the Last Will and Testament of the Late Robert

Richard Randall

Robert Richard Randall

Copy of the Last Will and Testament of the Late Robert Richard Randall

ISBN/EAN: 9783337306717

Printed in Europe, USA, Canada, Australia, Japan

Cover: Foto ©Thomas Meinert / pixelio.de

More available books at **www.hansebooks.com**

COPY

OF THE

LAST WILL AND TESTAMENT

OF THE LATE

ROBERT RICHARD RANDALL, ESQ.,

OF

THE ACT OF INCORPORATION,

AND OF THE OTHER ACTS OF THE LEGISLATURE OF THE
STATE OF NEW YORK,

RESPECTING THE

SAILORS' SNUG HARBOR:

TOGETHER WITH

THE NAMES OF THE PERSONS WHO HAVE ACTED AS TRUSTEES OF THE
SAME,—WITH THEIR BY-LAWS, &c.

PUBLISHED BY ORDER OF THE TRUSTEES.

NEW YORK:
SLOTE & JANES, STATIONERS & PRINTERS, 140 NASSAU STREET.

1883.

The Last Will and Testament

OF

ROBERT RICHARD RANDALL, Esq.

In the Name of God, Amen. I, ROBERT RICHARD
RANDALL, of the seventh ward of the city of New York,
being weak in body, but of sound and disposing mind and
memory, do make and ordain this my last Will and Testament, as follows :

FIRST. I direct all my just debts to be paid.

SECONDLY. I give unto the legitimate children of my
brother, Paul R. Randall, each an annuity or yearly sum
of forty pounds, until they respectively attain the age of
fifteen years ; and in addition thereto, I give to each of the
sons of my said brother, the sum of one thousand pounds,
to be paid to them as they may respectively attain the age
of twenty-one years ; and also to each daughter which my
said brother may have, the like sum of one thousand
pounds each, to be paid to them as they may respectively
be married.

THIRDLY. I give and bequeath unto Betsey Hart, my
housekeeper, my gold sleeve buttons, and an annuity or
yearly payment of forty pounds, to be paid her in quarterly
payments, during her natural life.

FOURTHLY. I give and bequeath unto Adam Shields, my faithful overseer, my gold watch and the sum of forty pounds, to be paid to him as soon after my decease as conveniently may be.

FIFTHLY. I also give and bequeath unto Gawn Irvin, who now lives with me, my shoe-buckles and knee-buckles, and also the sum of twenty pounds, to be paid immediately after my decease.

SIXTHLY. As to and concerning all the rest, residue and remainder of my estate, both real and personal, I give, devise and bequeath the same unto the Chancellor of the State of New York, the Mayor and Recorder of the city of New York, the President of the Chamber of Commerce in the city of New York, the President and Vice-President of the Marine Society of the city of New York, the senior Minister of the Episcopal Church in the said city, and the senior Minister of the Presbyterian Church in the said city ; to have and to hold all and singular the rest, residue and remainder of my said real and personal estate, unto them, the said Chancellor of the State of New York, Mayor of the city of New York, the Recorder of the city of New York, the President of the Chamber of Commerce, President and Vice-President of the Marine Society, senior Minister of the Episcopal Church, and senior Minister of the Presbyterian Church in the said city, for the time being, and their respective successors in the said offices, for ever, to, for and upon the uses, trusts, intents and purposes, and subject to the direction and appointments hereinafter mentioned and declared concerning the same ; that is to say, out of the rents, issues and profits of the said rest, residue and remainder of my said real add personal estate, to erect and build upon some eligible part of the land upon which I now reside, an Asylum, or Marine Hospital, to be called "The Sailors' Snug Harbor," for the purpose of maintaining and supporting aged, decrepit and worn-out sailors, as soon as they, my said charity Trustees, or a majority of

them, shall judge the proceeds of the said estate will support fifty of the said sailors, and upwards. And I do
hereby direct that the income of the said real and personal
estate, given as aforesaid to my said charity Trustees, shall
for ever hereafter be used and applied for supporting the
Asylum or Marine Hospital hereby directed to be built,
and for maintaining sailors of the above description therein,
in such manner as the said Trustees, or a majority of them,
may from time to time, or their successors in office may
from time to time, direct. And it is my intention that the
institution hereby directed and created should be perpetual,
and that the above-mentioned officers for the time being
and their successors, should for ever continue and be the
governors thereof, and have the superintendence of the
same ; and it is my will and desire that if it cannot legally
be done, according to my above intention, by them, without
an Act of the Legislature, it is my will and desire that they
will, as soon as possible, apply for an Act of the Legislature
to incorporate them for the purposes above specified. And
I do further declare it to be (my) will and intention that
the said rest, residue and remainder of my real and personal
estate should be, at all events, applied for the uses and
purposes above set forth ; and that it is my desire all courts
of law and equity will so construe this, my said Will, as to
have the said estate appropriated to the above uses, and
that the same should in no case, for want of legal form or
otherwise, be so construed as that my relations, or any
other persons, should heir, possess or enjoy my property,
except in the manner and for the uses herein above specified. And, lastly, I do nominate and appoint the Chancellor of the State of New York for the time being at the
time of my decease, the Mayor of the city of New York for
the time being, the Recorder of the city of New York for
the time being, the President of the Chamber of Commerce
for the time being, the President and Vice-President of the
Marine Society of the city of New York for the time being,
the senior Minister of the Episcopal Church in the city of
New York, and the senior Minister of the Presbyterian

Church in the said city, for the time being, and their successors in office after them, to be the executors of this my last Will and Testament, hereby revoking all former and other Wills, and declaring this to be my last Will and Testament.

In witness whereof I have hereunto set my hand and affixed my seal, the first day of June, in the year of our Lord one thousand eight hundred and one.

ROBERT RICHARD RANDALL. [L. S.]

Signed, sealed, published and declared by the said Testator as and for his last Will and Testament, in the presence of us, who in his presence, at his request, and in the presence of each other, have subscribed our names as witnesses thereto [there being an erasure from the word *President* to the end of the eleventh line of the second page].

URIAH BURDGE,
HENRY BREVOORT,
JONAS HUMBERT.

———

City and County of New York, ss. :

BE IT REMEMBERED, that on the tenth day of July, in the year of our Lord one thousand eight hundred and one, personally came and appeared before David Gelston, Surrogate of said County, Uriah Burdge, Henry Brevoort and Jonas Humbert, all of the said city, and being duly sworn on their oaths, declared that they saw Robert Richard Randall, deceased, sign and seal an Instrument in writing, purporting to be the Will of the said Robert Richard Randall, bearing date the first day of June, in the year of our Lord one thousand eight hundred and one (the pre-

ceding whereof is a true copy), and heard him publish and
declare the same as and for his last Will and Testament ;
that at the time thereof he, the said Robert Richard Randall, was of sound disposing mind and memory, to the best
of the knowledge and belief of them, the deponents ; and
that their names subscribed as witnesses to the said Will,
are of their own proper hands writing, which they respectively subscribed, as witnesses thereto, in the Testator's
presence.

DAVID GELSTON.

The preceding is a true copy of the original Will of
Robert Richard Randall, deceased, and of the Certificate of
the proof thereof.

SYLVANUS MILLER, *Surrogate.*

8

AN ACT

*To Incorporate the Trustees of the Marine Hospital, called
"THE SAILORS' SNUG HARBOR," in the City of New
York.*

Passed February 6, 1806.

WHEREAS, it is represented to the Legislature that
Robert Richard Randall, late of the city of New York,
deceased, in and by his last Will and Testament, duly made
and executed, bearing date the first day of June, in the year
of our Lord one thousand eight hundred and one, did,
after bequeathing certain specific legacies therein mentioned, among other things, give, devise and bequeath all
the residue of his estate, both real and personal, unto the
Chancellor of this State, the Mayor and Recorder of the city
of New York, the President of the Chamber of Commerce
in the city of New York, the President and Vice-President
of the Marine Society of the City of New York, the senior
Minister of the Episcopal Church in the said city, and the
senior Minister of the Presbyterian Church in the said city,
for the time being, and to their successors in office, respectively, in trust, to receive the rents, issues and profits thereof,
and to apply the same to the erecting or building, on some
eligible part of the land whereon the Testator then resided,
an Asylum or Marine Hospital, to be called The Sailors'
Snug Harbor, for the purpose of maintaining and supporting aged, decrepit and worn-out sailors, as soon as the said
Trustees, or a majority of them, should judge the proceeds
of the said estate would support fifty of such sailors,
and upwards; and that the said Testator, in his said
Will, declared his intention to be that the said estate
should at all events be applied to the purposes afore-

said, and no other : and if his said intent could not
be carried into effect without an act of incorporation, he
therein expressed his desire that his said Trustees would
apply to the Legislature for such incorporation. And
whereas the said Trustees have represented that the said
estate is of considerable value, and, if prudently managed,
will in time enable them to erect such Hospital, and carry
into effect the intent of the Testator ; but that as such
Trustees, and being also appointed executors of the said
Will in virtue of their offices, and only during their continuance in the said offices, they have found that considerable inconveniences have arisen in the management of the
said estate, from the changes which have taken place in the
ordinary course of the elections and appointments to those
offices, and have prayed to be incorporated for the purposes
expressed in the said Will, and such prayer appears to be
reasonable ; Therefore,

*Be it enacted by the People of the State of New York,
represented in Senate and Assembly,* That John Lansing,
junior, the Chancellor of this State ; De Witt Clinton, the
Mayor ; and Maturin Livingston, the Recorder of the city
of New York ; John Murray, the President of the Chamber
of Commerce in the city of New York ; James Farquhar,
the President, and Thomas Farmar, the first Vice-President
of the Marine Society of the city of New York ; Benjamin
Moore, senior Minister of the Episcopal Church in the said
city ; and John Rodgers, senior Minister of the Presbyterian
Church in the said city, and their successors in office
respectively, and in virtue of their said offices, shall be and
hereby are constituted and declared to be a body corporate,
in fact and in name, by the name and style of The Trustees
of the Sailors' Snug Harbor, in the city of New York, and
by that name they and their successors shall have continual
succession, and shall be capable in law of suing and being
sued, pleading and being impleaded, answering and being
answered unto, defending and being defended, in all courts
and places whatsoever, and in all manner of actions, suits,

complaints, matters and causes whatsoever, and that they and their successors may have a common seal, and may change and alter the same at their pleasure, and also that they and their successors, by the name and style aforesaid, shall be capable, in law, of holding and disposing of the said real and personal estate, devised and bequeathed as aforesaid, according to the intention of the said Will, and the same is hereby declared to be vested in them and their successors in office for the purposes therein expressed ; and shall also be capable of purchasing, holding and conveying any other real and personal estate, for the use and benefit of the said Corporation, in such manner as to them, or a majority of them, shall appear to be most conducive to the interest of the said institution.

And be it further enacted, That the said Trustees shall have power, from time to time, to make all proper and necessary rules and regulations for the government of the said Corporation, not inconsistent with the Constitution and laws of the United States and of this State, and to elect one of their number to be their President, and to appoint a Clerk and Treasurer, and such other officers as they may think proper, for the management of the business and concerns of the said Corporation, and to take and demand, if they shall deem it expedient, from every such Treasurer and other officers, such security for the faithful execution of their duty and the performance of the trust reposed in them respectively, as to the said Trustees shall seem proper ; and every bond or other security so taken by them shall be valid in law, and entitle the said Trustees to sue and recover thereon, according to the legal operation or effect thereof ; and the said officers shall respectively hold their offices during the pleasure of the said Trustees, and that any five or more of the said Trustees shall constitute a quorum to transact any of the business and concerns of the said Corporation.

And be it further enacted, That this Act shall be deemed

and taken to be a public Act, and be construed in all courts and places benignly and favorably for the purposes therein intended.

State of New York, Secretary's Office.

I certify the preceding to be a true copy of a certain original Act of our Legislature, now on file in this office (first sheet, first page, the words "*to receive,*" wrote on an erasure at the 12th line, and the word "*and,*" obliterated at the fifteenth line).

ELISHA JENKINS, Sec'ry.

Albany, 2d April, 1806.

AN ACT

To amend the Act entitled, "An Act to incorporate the Trustees of the Marine Hospital, called The Sailors' Snug Harbor, in the City of New York."

Passed March 25, 1814.

WHEREAS, the Trustees of the Sailors' Snug Harbor have represented that doubts exist as to who, in the contemplation of the Act of Incorporation, are to be considered the senior Ministers of the Episcopal and Presbyterian churches in the city of New York : Therefore,

Be it enacted by the People of the State of New York, represented in Senate and Assembly, That the Rector of Trinity Church, in the said city, or, in case of his sickness or absence, the assistant Rector of the said church, performing the functions of Rector, and the Minister of the Presbyterian Church in Wall street, in the said city, and in case there is more than one Minister in the said church, then the Minister first established in the said church, shall be the Trustees of the said Corporation.

And be it further enacted, That it shall be the duty of the said Corporation to make an annual Report to the Legislature, and to the Common Council of the city, of the state of their funds.

State of New York, Secretary's Office.

I certify the preceding to be a true copy of an original Act of the Legislature of this State, on file in this Office.

ARCH'D CAMPBELL, Dep. Sec'ry.

March 26th, 1814.

The property left by Captain Randall for the Sailors' Snug Harbor, consisted of land lying in the Fifteenth Ward of the city of New York, containing twenty-one acres, one rood, thirty-four perches, and one hundred and thirty-two feet ; also four lots in the First Ward of the city, together with seven hundred and twenty-three dollars in three per cent. stocks ; six thousand four hundred and thirty dollars in six per cent. stocks, and fifty shares of Manhattan stock.

It was the intention of the donor to have the Hospital built upon a part of the ground situated in the Fifteenth Ward. But in consequence of the rapid growth of the city, and of the great rise in the value of property within its limits, and also considering the habits and character of seamen, the Trustees became fully convinced that the benevolent design of the testator would be more extensively carried into effect by reserving the whole of the ground in their possession as a source of revenue for the support of the Institution ; and that the taste of the subjects of the charity would be more gratified, and their comfort greatly promoted, by purchasing a site for the Hospital on the margin of the East or North River, or in the vicinity thereof. They accordingly, in June, 1825, addressed a Memorial to the Legislature, requesting permission to improve and lease out their ground in the city, and to locate the Institution elsewhere. In April, 1828, the Legislature granted their request, and passed an Act, of which the following is a copy, viz. :—

COPY OF AN ACT further to amend an Act entitled "*An Act to Incorporate the Trustees of the Marine Hospital, called the Sailors' Snug Harbor, in the city of New York,*" passed March 25th, 1814.

Passed April 19th, 1828.

The People of the State of New York, represented in Senate and Assembly, do enact as follows :—

The Trustees of the Sailors' Snug Harbor in the city of New York are hereby authorized to adopt all such mea-

14

sures as may be necessary to regulate the tract of land devised to them by the last will and testament of Robert Richard Randall, so as to make it conform to the permanent plan of the city, and for that purpose the said Trustees may dig down their ground where it is too high, and remove it to other parts of the said premises which are too low ; and, further, that it shall be lawful for the said Trustees to sell and dispose of their surplus earth. The said Trustees shall be, and hereby are, authorized to purchase a suitable and convenient tract of ground, lying upon the island of New York, or adjacent thereto, and fronting upon the North or East River, or in the vicinity thereof, upon which it shall be lawful for the Trustees to build and erect a Marine Hospital, to be called and known for ever as The Sailors' Snug Harbor.

In the main or centre building shall be placed a suitable statue of Robert Richard Randall, with an inscription designating him as the munificent donor thereof. But that such ground shall not be purchased by the said Trustees for the purpose aforesaid until the approbation of the Court of Chancery be first had and obtained.

So soon as a suitable site for such Marine Hospital shall be purchased with the approbation of the Court of Chancery, it shall be lawful for the said Trustees to lease all the lots now belonging to the Sailors' Snug Harbor on such terms and conditions, and under such covenants, as they may deem most beneficial for the interests thereof.

The Sailors' Snug Harbor, or the Trustees in behalf thereof, may take, hold and enjoy in fee simple for ever, any lands, tenements or other property which may be devised to them, notwithstanding they be a body corporate.

State of New York, Secretary's Office.

I certify the preceding to be a true copy of an original law on file in this office.

Signed,   ARCH'D CAMPBELL,
                                       Deputy Secretary.

Albany, 21st April, 1828.

In pursuance of the foregoing Act, the Trustees proceeded to regulate their ground in the Fifteenth Ward, making it conformable to the plan of the city, and to lease the same for the term of twenty-one years, with the privilege of renewal as specified in the leases given, a copy of which will be found in a subsequent page.

They also visited different sites in the vicinity of the city, and on the margin of the waters of our bay and rivers, which were offered for sale at the time, and examined the same with reference to the proposed hospital.

In May, 1831, they purchased the farm on Staten Island, now known as the Sailor's Snug Harbor, containing one-hundred and thirty acres of excellant land, eligibly situated and well watered. They have since purchased twenty additional acres of land adjoining, and having been originally a part of the same farm.

On the eleventh of October, 1831, the corner-stone of the Sailors' Snug Harbor was laid.

On that occasion, and in the presence of several officers of the State government, and of a large number of respectable citizens, the acting president of the Board, Walter Bowne, Esq., briefly stated the object of the meeting ; Rev. Dr. Berrian offered the introductory prayer ; the Hon. Reuben H. Walworth delivered an appropriate address and laid the corner-stone ; the Rev. Dr. Phillips offered the concluding prayer.

On the first of August, 1833, the institution was formally opened with the following exercises, viz. : introductory prayer by the Rev. Dr. Van Pelt ; an address to the aged, decrepit and worn-out seamen, who had been received under the care of the Board, by the Rev. Dr. Phillips, and a concluding prayer by the Rev. J. E. Miller.

The remains of Captain Randall were removed, under the direction of the Board, and deposited beneath a marble monument in front of the building, on the 21st of August,

1834. The following is a copy of the inscriptions on the same, viz. :

North Side.

The Trustees of the Sailors' Snug Harbor erected this Monument
To the memory of
ROBERT RICHARD RANDALL,
By whose Munificence this Institution was Founded.

East Side.

The Humane Institution of the Sailors' Snug Harbor,
Conceived in a spirit of enlarged Benevolence,
With an Endowment which time has proved fully adequate to the objects
of the Donor ;
And organized in a manner which shows
Wisdom and Foresight.
The Founder of this noble Charity
Will ever be held in grateful Remembrance
By the partakers of his Bounty.

South Side.

Charity never Faileth.
Its Memorial is Immortal.

West Side.

The Trustees of the Sailors' Snug Harbor caused the remains of
ROBERT RICHARD RANDALL
To be removed from the original place of Interment
And deposited beneath this Monument,
On the 21st of August, 1834.

A marble bust of Mr. Randall has also been procured and placed in the hall of the centre building.

The public buildings of the Snug Harbor on Staten Island consist at present of a centre or main building, with two wings, a dining-hall building, a hospital and chapel. An additional building for the accommodation of inmates, also a kitchen, are now being erected.

The income of the property belonging to the Sailors' Snug Harbor—which in 1806 amounted to four thousand two hundred and forty-three dollars—amounts now to about two hundred thousand dollars, showing an increase in the value of property, and furnishing evidence of a wise and judicious investment of funds, and of faithful management of the same, and above all, of a kind and careful Providence over this institution, almost without a parallel in the history of public charities and of public trusts.

The following persons have been acting Trustees of the Sailors' Snug Harbor since the incorporation of the Board in 1806, some continuing in office a longer and others a shorter period of time:

1. *As Chancellor*—REUBEN H. WALWORTH.

By the new Constitution of the State of New-York—adopted 3d November, 1846—the office of Chancellor was abolished from and after the 1st Monday of July, 1847. Since that time the Board of Trustees has been deprived of the valuable services of the Hon. Reuben H. Walworth; and the Board now consists of seven members.

2. *As Mayors of the City of New York*—De Witt Clinton, Marinus Willet, John Ferguson, Jacob Radcliff, Cadwallader D. Colden, Stephen Allen, Wm. Paulding, Philip Hone, Walter Bowne, Gideon Lee, Cornelius W. Lawrence, Aaron Clark, Isaac L. Varian, Robert H. Morris, Wm. F. Havemeyer, James Harper, Andrew H. Mickle, Wm. V. Brady, Wm. F. Havemeyer, Caleb S. Woodhull, Ambrose C. Kingsland, Jacob A. Westervelt, Fernando Wood, Daniel F. Tiemann, George Opdyke, Godfrey Gunther, John T. Hoffman, Thomas Coman, A. Oakey Hall, William F. Havemeyer, William H. Wickham.

3. *As Recorders of the City of New York*—Pierre C. Van Wyck, Josiah Ogden Hoffman, Richard Riker, Peter Augustus Jay, Robert H. Morris, Frederick A. Tallmadge, John B. Scott, Frederick A. Tallmadge, Francis R. Tillou, James M. Smith, Jr., George G. Barnard, John T. Hoffman, John K. Hackett.

4. *As Presidents of the Chamber of Commerce*—Cornelius Ray, Wm. Bayard, Robert Lenox, Isaac Carow, James De Peyster Ogden, James G. King, Moses H. Grinnell, James

G. King, Moses H. Grinnell, Elias Hicks, Pelatiah Perit, A. A. Low, William E. Dodge, Samuel D. Babcock.

5. *As Presidents of the Marine Society*—James Farquhar, John Whetten, Charles A. Marshall, John M. Ferrier, William C. Thompson.

6. *As Vice-Presidents of the Marine Society*—Thos. Farmar, Wm. Whitlock, James Lovitt, Thomas H. Merry, William Thomson, Jeremiah Dickenson, John M. Ferrier, Thomas Dunham, Ambrose Snow.

7. *As Senior Ministers and Rectors of Trinity Church*—Benjamin Moore, D.D., John Hervey Hobart, D.D., Wm. Berrian, D.D., Morgan Dix, D.D.

8. *As Ministers of the First Presbyterian Church in Wall Street*—John Rodgers, D.D., Philip Melancthon Whelpley, Wm. W. Phillips, D.D., Wm. M. Paxton, D.D.

The officers of the Board, as at present organized, are : Ambrose Snow, President ; Thomas Greenleaf, Secretary; Thomas Greenleaf, Controller.

Executive Committee—Ambrose Snow, Chairman ; Rev. Wm. M. Paxton, Samuel D. Babcock.

Officers of the Institution—Thomas Melville, Governor ; Joseph K. Clark, Steward; Rev. Charles J. Jones, Resident Chaplain ; Dr. S. V. R. Bogert, Resident Physician ; Samuel Cobb, Agent.

The apparent delay to carry into effect the design of the donor of this charity, was occasioned in the first instance by the very limited income of the estate, and subsequently by the great expense necessarily incurred in defending suits brought against the Trustees by different claimants for the property; by the consequent unsettled state of the trust, and the difficulty of leasing the ground while those attempts to set aside the Will were making ; and by the heavy assessments and the payment of certain quit-rents which became necessary in regulating the lots and opening streets through the same.

It was not until March, 1830, that the last suit brought

against the Trustees, by persons claiming to be heirs of Mr. Randall, was finally and forever settled by the Supreme Court of the United States. Since then, as the history of their proceedings will show, the Trustees have been diligently engaged in improving the property left in their charge, and in promoting the benevolent designs of the Testator. They have now under their care, and in successful operation, an institution containing about five hundred inmates, who are comfortably yet economically fed and clothed, and have all their necessary wants supplied. Their religious instruction is attended to, conceding to all, however, liberty of conscience.

Public worship is regularly conducted on the Sabbath in the chapel building. There is also in the institution, and for the use of the inmates, a carefully selected Library and Reading-room, where several of the daily and weekly newspapers of the City of New York are received.

The form of lease on renewal of the old leases given in 1827.

This Indenture, Made this   day of
in the year of our Lord one thousand eight hundred and
          BETWEEN "The Trustees of the SAILORS' SNUG
HARBOR, in the City of New York," of the first part, and
          of the second part: WHEREAS the said parties of
the first part, by Indenture dated the   day of
in the year one thousand eight hundred and   did
grant and demise unto   all that certain lot of land
hereinafter described for the term of   years from the
          day of   then next, subject to certain rents,
covenants and conditions therein reserved and expressed.
And among other things it was thereby agreed that in case
of the erection on the said lot of land of a building of such
description as is therein specified, the said parties of the
first part should, at the expiration of the said term, either
pay for the said building according to the appraised value
thereof, or grant a new lease of the said lot for the further
term of twenty-one years, at a reasonable rent, to be ascertained as is therein mentioned. AND WHEREAS a building
has been erected on the said lot of land of the description
mentioned in the said lease; and the said parties of the
first part having elected to renew the same for such further
term, and the said part   hereto of the second part being
now possessed of the said first mentioned lease, it has been
mutually agreed by and between the parties hereto, that
the rent to be paid on the said lot of land for and during
such new term, shall be that hereinafter reserved.

Now this Indenture Witnesseth, that "THE TRUSTEES
OF THE SAILORS' SNUG HARBOR, IN THE CITY OF NEW
YORK," the said parties hereto of the first part, in consideration of the rents and covenants hereinafter reserved and
contained, have granted, demised, and to farm let, and by
these presents, Do grant, demise, and to farm let, unto the

said part   of the second part, ALL   certain Lot
of Land, situate, lying and being in the   Ward of
the city of New York ; being part of the lands of the said
parties of the first part, and distinguished in

𝕿𝖔 𝖍𝖆𝖛𝖊 𝖆𝖓𝖉 𝖙𝖔 𝖍𝖔𝖑𝖉 the said Lot of Land, unto the said
part of   of the second part,   executors, administrators, and assigns, from the   day of
for and during, and until the full end and term of
years thence next ensuing, and fully to be complete and
ended ; yielding and paying for the same, yearly and every
year during the said term, unto the said parties of the first
part, their successors or assigns. the sum of   dollars, of lawful money of the United States, in two equal
half-yearly payments ; that is to say, on the first day of
May and on the first day of November, in each and every
year, during the term hereby granted ; the first payment to
be made on the first day of   now next ensuing.
SUBJECT NEVERTHELESS to all such taxes, assessments and
incumbrances (if any) as may have been assessed, imposed
or charged on the said demised premises, or any part
thereof, since the date of the said first recited Indenture.
PROVIDED ALWAYS, that if it shall happen that the said
yearly rent, or any part thereof, shall not be paid on any
day on which the same ought to be paid, as aforesaid, then,
and at all times thereafter, it shall and may be lawful to
and for the said parties of the first part, their successors or
assigns, into the said demised premises, or any part thereof,
in the name of the whole, to re-enter, and to re-possess,
have and enjoy the same again, as of their first and former
estate and interest therein ; anything herein contained to
the contrary in anywise nothwithstanding. And the said
part   of the second part, for   executors, administrators and assigns, do   hereby   covenant and
agree, to and with the said parties of the first part, their
successors and assigns, that the said part   of the second
part,   executors, administrators and assigns, shall
and will, half yearly, and every year during the term hereby

granted, well and truly pay unto the said parties of the first part, their successors or assigns, the said rent hereby reserved, at the days and times hereinbefore limited for the payment thereof, without fraud or delay. AND ALSO, that the said part   of the second part,   executors, administrators or assigns, shall and will, at   own proper costs and charges, bear, pay and discharge all such duties, taxes, assessments and payments, extraordinary as well as ordinary, as shall, during the term hereby granted, be imposed, or grow due and payable, out of, or for, the said demised premises, or any part thereof, by virtue of any present or future law of the United States of America, or of the State of New York, or of the Corporation of the City of New York: AND ALSO, that the said part   of the second part,   executors, administrators or assigns, or any of them, shall not, nor will, at any time or times hereafter during the term hereby granted, lease, let or demise all or any part of the said premises, nor assign, transfer or make over the same, or this present lease, or any of   term or time therein, to any person or persons whomsoever, without the consent of the said parties of the first part, their successors or assigns, in writing under their seal for that purpose first had and obtained, anything hereinbefore contained to the contrary thereof in anywise notwithstanding. AND ALSO, that the said part of the second part,   executors, administrators or assigns, or any of them, shall not, nor will, at any time hereafter, during the term hereby granted, erect, make, establish or carry on, nor cause or suffer to be erected, made, established or carried on, in any manner, or any part of the above-described and hereby demised premises, any stable, slaughter house, tallow chandlery, smith shop, forge, furnace, or brass foundry, nail or other iron factory, or any manufactory for the making of glass, starch, glue, varnish, vitriol, turpentine, or ink; or for tanning, dressing, preparing or keeping skins, hides or leather; or any distillery, brewery, sugar bakery, or any other manufactory, trade, business or calling whatsoever, which may be

in anywise noxious or offensive to the neighboring inhabitants. AND, LASTLY, that the said part   of the second
part,   executors, administrators or assigns shall
and will, on the last day of the term hereby granted, or
other sooner determination thereof, well and truly surrender and deliver up the said hereby demised premises into
the possession of the said parties of the first part, their successors or assigns, without fraud or delay. PROVIDED
ALWAYS, that it shall be lawful for the said parties of the
first part, their successors and assigns, when and as often
as default shall be made in the payment of the said rent, or
any part thereof, to take such summary proceedings for the
recovery of the said rent as may be permitted by law, anything herein contained notwithstanding. AND PROVIDED
FURTHER, *and this present lease is upon this express condition*, That if the said part   of the second part,   executors, administrators or assigns, shall, at any time during
the term hereby granted, erect, make, establish or carry on
or cause or suffer to be erected, made, established or carried
on, in any manner, on any part of the above described and
hereby demised premises, any stable, slaughter house, tallow chandlery, smith shop, forge, furnace, or brass foundry,
nail or other iron factory, or any manufactory for the making of glass, starch, glue, varnish, vitriol, turpentine or ink;
or for tanning, dressing, preparing, or keeping skins, hides,
or leather ; or any distillery, brewery, sugar bakery, or any
other manufactory, trade, business or calling whatsoever,
which may be in anywise noxious or offensive to the neighboring inhabitants, or shall fail in the performance of any
or either of the covenants, conditions or provisoes in these
presents contained, which on the part and behalf of the
said part   of the second part,   executors, administrators and assigns, are, or ought to be, observed, performed, fulfilled and kept, then and from thenceforth, this
present Indenture and the Estate hereby granted, and every
clause, article and thing herein contained on the part
and behalf of the said parties of the first part, to be performed, fulfilled and kept, shall cease, determine and be

utterly void, to all intents and purposes whatsoever, anything herein contained to the contrary thereof in anywise notwithstanding.

AND it is hereby mutually covenanted and agreed, that at the expiration of the term hereby granted, if the said parties hereto shall agree upon a renewal of this lease for a further term of twenty-one years, and shall, by mutual consent, fix upon the annual ground rent to be reserved in such renewed lease, and which shall not be less than the rent herein reserved, then the said parties of the first part, their successors or assigns, shall and will execute to the said part   of the said part,   executors, administrators or assigns, at   expense, a new lease of the aforesaid premises for the term of twenty-one years, from and after the expiration of the term hereby demised, at the annual ground rent, payable half-yearly, agreed upon between the said parties as aforesaid. But if at the expiration of the term hereby granted, the said parties shall not agree upon a renewal of this lease, or upon the amount of the rent to be reserved for such renewed term, then each party shall choose a disinterested person, who shall be the owner in fee simple of one or more lots of land in the neighborhood of the premises hereby demised, and the said persons so chosen shall, under oath, appraise the land hereby demised, considering it as a vacant lot, at its full and fair worth at private sale ; and they shall also, under oath, appraise the house now erected on the said lot, or any other house of like description as its substitute, which shall cover the whole front of such lot—be constructed of brick or stone,   or more stories high—and covered with slate or metal, with its front finished in such style as may be approved of by the said parties of the first part, their successors or assigns, at its then actual worth, without reference to the ground on which it stands ; and in case the said appraisers shall differ in their valuation or appraisement, either of the lot or building, they shall then choose an umpire, qualified as aforesaid, whose decision, under oath, shall be final and conclusive.

AND the said parties of the first part, their successors or assigns, shall have the full liberty and choice, either to pay to the said part   of the second part,   executors, administrators or assigns, the value of the said building so determined as aforesaid, or to grant a renewal of this lease unto the said part   of the second part,   executors, administrators or assigns, at   their expense, for the term of twenty-one years from and after the expiration cf the term hereby granted, at an annual ground rent of five per cent. on the valuation of the said lot so determined as aforesaid, but not less than the rent hereby reserved.

AND it is further mutually covenanted and agreed, that at the expiration of the term to be granted by the first renewal of this lease, and at the expiration of each and every term which may be thereafter granted by each and every subsequent renewal of this lease, the said parties of the first part, their successors or assigns, shall still have and retain the full liberty and choice, either to grant a further renewal, for the further term of twenty-one years, at such annual rent, payable half-yearly (but not less than the rent of the last preceding term), as shall be ascertained and determined in the manner aforesaid, or to pay unto the said part   of the second part,   executors, administrators or assigns, the value of the said

to be ascertained as aforesaid. And it is further mutually covenanted and agreed, by and between the parties aforesaid, that whenever the said parties of the first part, their successors or assigns, shall refuse to grant a renewal of this lease as aforesaid, the said   shall be valued and paid for as aforesaid : PROVIDED ALWAYS, that the part of the second part,   executors, administrators or assigns, shall not be compelled to surrender the premises until such payment be made or tendered. And it is further mutually covenanted and agreed, by and between the parties aforesaid, that in case the said parties of the first part, their successors or assigns, shall, at the expiration of the term to be granted by this lease, or at the expiration of any term which may be granted thereafter, by any subsequent renewal thereof, elect and choose to pay unto the said part   of the second part,   executors, administrators or assigns, the value of the said   to be ascertained as aforesaid, and shall actually make such payment, or tender the same, the said part   of the second part,   executors, administrators or assigns, shall then deliver up the said   in the same order and condition in which it was at the time of its valuation, as aforesaid, and also all and singular other the premises hereby demised, to the said parties of the first part, their successors or assigns, without fraud or delay. AND LASTLY, it is mutually covenanted and agreed, by and between the parties aforesaid, that each renewed lease shall contain the like covenants, provisoes and conditions as herein contained.

In Witness whereof, the said parties of the first part have caused their seal to be affixed hereto ; and the said part of the second part *ha*   set   hand and seal interchangeably, the day and year first above written.

The form of lease on renewal of the leases given in and after 1830, according to the form adopted by the Trustees at that time.

𝕿𝖍𝖎𝖘 𝕴𝖓𝖉𝖊𝖓𝖙𝖚𝖗𝖊, Made this   day of   , in the year of our Lord one thousand eight hundred and   Between "The Trustees of The SAILORS' SNUG HARBOR, in the City of New York," of the first part, and   of the second part : WHEREAS, the said parties of the first part, by Indenture dated the   day of in the year one thousand eight hundred and   did grant and demise unto   all that certain lot of land hereinafter described for the term of   years from the   day of   then next, subject to certain rents, covenants and conditions therein reserved and expressed. And among other things it was thereby agreed that in case of the erection on the said lot of land of a building of such description as is therein specified, the said parties of the first part should, at the expiration of the said term, grant a new lease of the said lot for the further term of twenty-one years, at an annual rent to be agreed upon or ascertained as is therein mentioned ; and with such covenants, conditions and provisoes to be therein inserted as are hereinafter contained. AND WHEREAS, a building has been erected on the said lot of land of the description mentioned in the said lease, according to the terms thereof, whereby the said part   of the second part,   entitled to a renewal of the said lease for such further term, at an annual rent hereinafter reserved, and now   in the manner prescribed by the said lease, payable half-yearly, and subject to the covenants, conditions and provisoes hereinafter contained.

𝕹𝖔𝖜 𝖙𝖍𝖎𝖘 𝕴𝖓𝖉𝖊𝖓𝖙𝖚𝖗𝖊 𝖂𝖎𝖙𝖓𝖊𝖘𝖘𝖊𝖙𝖍, that "THE TRUSTEES OF THE SAILORS' SNUG HARBOR, IN THE CITY OF NEW YORK," the said parties hereto of the first part, in consideration of the rents and covenants hereinafter reserved and contained, have granted, demised and to farm let, and by these presents, Do grant, demise, and to farm let, unto the said part   of the second part, ALL   certain lot of land, situate, lying and being in the   Ward of the city of New York; being part of the land of the said parties of the first part, and distinguished in

𝕿𝖔 𝖍𝖆𝖛𝖊 𝖆𝖓𝖉 𝖙𝖔 𝖍𝖔𝖑𝖉 the said Lot of Land, unto the said part   of the second part,   executors, administrators and assigns, from the   day of   for and during, and until the full end and term of   years thence next ensuing, and fully to be complete and ended ; yielding and paying for the same, yearly and every year during the said term, unto the said parties of the first part, their successors or assigns, the sum of   dollars, of lawful money of the United States, in two equal half-yearly payments ; that is to say, on the first day of May, and on the first day of November, in each and every year during the term hereby granted, the first payment to be made on the first day of   now next ensuing. SUBJECT NEVERTHELESS to all such taxes, assessments and incumbrances (if any) as may have been assessed, imposed or charged on the said demised premises, or any part thereof, since the date of the said first recited Indenture. PROVIDED ALWAYS, that if it shall happen that the said yearly rent, or any part thereof, shall not be paid on any date on which the same ought to be paid, as aforesaid, then, and at all times thereafter, it shall and may be lawful to and for the said parties of the first part, their successors or assigns, into the said demised premises, or any part thereof, in the name of the whole, to re-enter and to re-possess, have and enjoy the same again, as of their first and former estate and interest therein, anything herein contained to the contrary in anywise notwithstanding. And the said part   of the second part, for   executors, administrators and assigns, do hereby   covenant and agree, to and with the said parties of the first part, their successors and assigns,

that the said part   of the second part,   executors,
administrators and assigns, shall and will, half-yearly, and
every year during the term hereby granted, well and truly
pay unto the said parties of the first part, their successors
or assigns, the said rent hereby reserved, at the days and
times hereinbefore limited for the payment thereof, without
fraud or delay. AND ALSO, that the said part   of the
second part,   executors, administrators or assigns,
shall and will, at   own proper costs and charges,
bear, pay, and discharge all such duties, taxes, assessments
and payments, extraordinary as well as ordinary, as shall,
during the term hereby granted, be imposed, or grow due
and payable, out of, or for, the said demised premises,
or any part thereof, by virtue or any present or future law
of the United States of America, or of the State of New
York, or of the Corporation of the City of New York. AND
ALSO, that the said part   of the second part,
executors, administrators or assigns, or any of them, shall
not, nor will, at any time or times hereafter, during the
term hereby granted, lease, let or demise all or any part of
the said premises, nor assign, transfer or make over the
same, or this present lease, or any of   term or time
therein, to any person or persons whomsoever, without the
consent of the said parties of the first part, their successors
or assigns, in writing under their seal for that purpose first
had and obtained, anything hereinbefore contained to the
contrary thereof in any wise notwithstanding. AND ALSO,
that the said part   of the second part,   executors,
administrators or assigns, or any of them, shall not, nor
will, at any time hereafter, during the term hereby granted,
erect, make, establish or carry on, nor cause or suffer to be
erected, made, established or carried on, in any manner, on
any part of the above described and hereby demised premises, any stable, slaughter house, tallow chandlery, smith
shop, forge, furnace, or brass foundry, nail or other iron
factory, or any manufactory for the making of glass, starch,
glue, varnish, vitriol, turpentine or ink ; or for tanning,
dressing, preparing or keeping skins, hides or leather ; or

any distillery, brewery, sugar bakery, or any other manufactory, trade, business or calling whatsoever, which may
be in anywise noxious or offensive to the neighboring
inhabitants. AND LASTLY, that the said part   of the
second part,   executors, administrators or assigns,
shall and will, on the last day of the term hereby granted,
or other sooner determination thereof, well and truly surrender and deliver up the said hereby demised premises
into the possession of the said parties of the first part, their
successors or assigns, without fraud or delay. PROVIDED
ALWAYS, that it shall be lawful for the said parties of the
first part, their successors and assigns, when and as often
as default shall be made in the payment of the said rent, or
any part thereof, to take such summary proceedings for the
recovery of the said rent as may be permitted by law, anything herein contained to the contrary notwithstanding.
AND PROVIDED FURTHER, *and this present lease is upon
this express condition*, That if the said part   of the
second part,   executors, administrators or assigns,
shall at any time during the term hereby granted, erect,
make, establish or carry on, or cause, or suffer to be erected,
made, established or carried on, in any manner, on any part
of the above described and hereby demised premises, any
stable, slaughter house, tallow chandlery, smith shop, forge,
furnace or brass foundry, nail or other iron factory, or any
manufactory for the making of glass, starch, glue, varnish,
vitriol, turpentine or ink ; or for tanning, dressing, preparing or keeping skins, hides or leather ; or any distillery,
brewery, sugar bakery, or any other manufactory, trade,
business or calling whatsoever, which may be in anywise
noxious or offensive to the neighboring inhabitants, or shall
fail in the performance of any or either of the covenants,
conditions or provisoes in these presents contained, which on
the part and behalf of the said part   of the second part,
            executors, administrators and assigns, are, or
ought to be, observed, performed, fulfilled and kept, then
and from thenceforth, this present Indenture and the Estate
hereby granted, and every clause, article and thing herein

contained, on the part and behalf of the said parties of the
first part, to be performed, fulfilled and kept, shall cease,
determine and be utterly void, to all intents and purposes
whatsoever, anything herein contained to the contrary thereof in anywise notwithstanding.

AND it is hereby mutually covenanted and agreed, that
at the expiration of the term hereby granted, if the said
parties hereto shall agree upon a renewal of this lease for a
further term of twenty-one years, and shall, by mutual consent, fix upon the annual ground rent to be reserved in
such renewed lease, and which shall not be less than the
rent herein reserved, then the said parties of the first part,
their successors or assigns, shall, and will, execute to the
said part   of the second part,   executors, administrators or assigns, at   expense, a new lease of the
aforesaid premises for the term of twenty-one years, from
and after the expiration of the term hereby demised, at the
annual ground rent, payable half-yearly, agreed upon between the same parties as aforesaid. But if, at the expiration of the term hereby granted, the said parties shall not
agree upon a renewal of this lease, or upon the amount of
the rent to be reserved for such renewed term, then each
party shall choose a disinterested person, who shall be the
owner in fee simple of one or more lots of land in the
neighborhood of the premises hereby demised, and the said
persons so chosen shall, under oath, appraise the land
hereby demised, considering it as a vacant lot, and its full
and fair worth at private sale ; and they shall also, under
oath, appraise, the house now erected on the said lot, or
any other house of like description as its substitute, which
shall cover the whole front of such lot—be constructed of
brick or stone,   or more stories high—and covered
with slate or metal, with its front finished in such style as
may be approved of by the said parties of the first part,
their successors or assigns, at its then actual worth, without
reference to the ground on which it stands ; and in case the
said appraisers shall differ in their valuation or appraisement, either of the lot or building, they shall then choose

an umpire, qualified as aforesaid, whose decision, under oath, shall be final and conclusive.

AND the said parties of the first part, their successors or assigns, shall have the full liberty and choice, either to pay to the said part   of the second part,   executors, administrators or assigns, the value of the said building so determined as aforesaid, or to grant a renewal of this lease unto the said part   of the second part,   executors, administrators or assigns, at   their expense, for the term of twenty-one years from and after the expiration of the term hereby granted, at an annual ground rent of five per cent. on the valuation of the said lot so determined as aforesaid, but not less than the rent hereby reserved.

AND it is further mutually covenanted and agreed, that at the expiration of the term to be granted by the first renewal of this lease, and at the expiration of each and every term which may be thereafter granted by each and every subsequent renewal of this lease, the said parties of the first part, their successors or assigns, shall still have and retain the full liberty and choice, either to grant a further renewal, for the further term of twenty-one years, at such annual rent, payable half-yearly (but not less than the rent of the last preceding term), as shall be ascertained and determined in the manner aforesaid, or to pay unto the said part   of the second part,   executors, administrators or assigns, the value of the said
to he ascertained as aforesaid.   And it is further mutually covenanted and agreed, by and between the parties aforesaid, that whenever the said parties of the first part, their successors or assigns, shall refuse to grant a renewal of this lease as aforesaid, the said
                    shall be valued and paid for as aforesaid. PROVIDED ALWAYS, that the part   of the second part,   executors, administrators or assigns, shall not be compelled to surrender the premises until such payment be made or tendered.   And it is further mutually covenanted and agreed, by and between the parties aforesaid, that in case the said parties of the first part, their successors or

assigns, shall, at the expiration of the term to be granted by this lease, or at the expiration of any term which may be granted hereafter, by any subsequent renewal thereof, elect and choose to pay unto the said part   of the second part,   executors, administrators or assigns, the value of the said
to be ascertained as aforesaid, and shall actually make such payment, or tender the same, the said part   of the second part,   executors, administrators or assigns, shall then deliver up the said

in the same order and condition in which it was at the time of its valuation, as aforesaid, and also all and singular other the premises hereby demised, to the said parties of the first part, their successors or assigns, without fraud or delay. AND LASTLY, it is mutually covenanted and agreed, by and between the parties aforesaid, that each renewed lease shall contain the like covenants, provisoes and conditions as herein contained.

In Witness whereof, the said parties of the first part have caused their seal to be affixed hereto; and the said part of the second part, ha   set   hand and seal interchangeably, the day and year first above written.

2. The lessees or sub-lessees shall pay all expenses and charges for leases, transfers and acknowledgements of the same.

The form of lease on renewal of the leases given in and since 1873.

𝕿𝖍𝖎𝖘 𝕴𝖓𝖉𝖊𝖓𝖙𝖚𝖗𝖊, Made this   day of   , in the year of our Lord one thousand eight hundred and
          Between "The Trustees of The SAILORS' SNUG HARBOR, in the City of New York," of the first part, and
          of the second part: WHEREAS, the said parties of the first part, by Indenture of Lease, dated the   day of
          in the year one thousand eight hundred and
did grant and demise unto   all that certain lot of land hereinafter described for the term of   years from the   day of   , subject to certain rents, covenants and conditions therein reserved and expressed. AND WHEREAS, the said parties of the first part, and the said part   of the second part, the latter claiming to be the present owner   of said Indenture of Lease, have agreed upon a renewal thereof, for a further term of twenty-one years, at the annual rent hereinafter reserved, payable half-yearly, and subject to the covenants, conditions and provisoes hereinafter contained.

𝕹𝖔𝖜 𝖙𝖍𝖎𝖘 𝕴𝖓𝖉𝖊𝖓𝖙𝖚𝖗𝖊 𝖂𝖎𝖙𝖓𝖊𝖘𝖘𝖊𝖙𝖍, that "THE TRUSTEES OF THE SAILORS' SNUG HARBOR, IN THE CITY OF NEW YORK," the said parties hereto of the first part, in consideration of the rents and covenants hereinafter reserved and contained, have granted, demised and to farm let, and by these presents, Do grant, demise, and to farm let, unto the said part   of the second part, ALL that certain lot of land, situate, lying and being in the   Ward of the city of New York; being part of the land of the said parties of the first part, and distinguished on a map of their property in the said Ward, made by EDWIN SMITH, City Surveyor, dated April 13th, 1848, and filed in the office of the Register of the city and county of New York, by the Number

𝕿𝖔 𝖍𝖆𝖛𝖊 𝖆𝖓𝖉 𝖙𝖔 𝖍𝖔𝖑𝖉 the said Lot of Land, unto the said part   of the second part,   executors, adminis-trators and assigns, from the   for and during, and until the full end and term of   years thence next ensuing, and fully to be complete and ended ; yield-ing and paying for the same, yearly and every year during the said term, unto the said parties of the first part, their successors or assigns, the sum of   dollars, of law-ful money of the United States, in two equal half-yearly payments ; that is to say, on the first day of May, and on the first day of November, in each and every year during the term hereby granted, the first payment to be made on the first day of   now next ensuing. SUBJECT NEVER-THELESS to all such taxes, assessments and incumbrances (if any) as may have been assessed, imposed or charged on the said demised premises, or any part thereof, since the date of the said first recited Indenture, or since the date of the Indenture therein recited. PROVIDED ALWAYS, that if it shall happen that the said yearly rent, or any part thereof, shall not be paid on any day on which the same ought to be paid, as aforesaid, then, and at all times thereafter, it shall and may be lawful to and for the said parties of the first part, their successors or assigns, into the said demised premises, or any part thereof, in the name of the whole, to re-enter and re-possess, have and enjoy the same again, as of their first and former estate and interest therein, anything herein contained to the contrary in anywise notwithstanding. And the said part   of the second part, for   executors, administrators and assigns, do   hereby covenant and agree, to and with the said parties of the first part, their successors and assigns, that the said part   of the second part,   executors, administrators and assigns, shall and will, half-yearly, and every year during the term hereby granted, well and truly pay unto the said parties of the first part, their successors or assigns, the said rent hereby reserved, at the days and times hereinbefore limited for the payment thereof, without fraud or delay. AND ALSO, that the said part   of the

second part,   executors, administrators or assigns, shall
and will, at   their own proper costs and charges,
bear, pay, and discharge all such duties, taxes, assessments
and payments, extraordinary as well as ordinary, as shall,
during the term hereby granted, be imposed, or grow due
and payable, out of, or for, the said demised premises, or
any part thereof, by virtue of any present or future law of
the United States of America, or of the State of New
York, or of the Corporation of the City of New York. AND
ALSO, that the said part   of the second part,
executors, administrators or assigns, or any of them, shall
not, nor will, at any time or times hereafter, during the
term hereby granted, lease, let or demise all or any part of
the said premises, nor assign, transfer or make over the same,
or this present lease, or any of   their term or time
therein, to any person or persons whomsoever, without the
consent of the said parties of the first part, their successors
or assigns, in writing under their seal for that purpose first
had and obtained, anything hereinbefore contained to the
contrary thereof in any wise notwithstanding. AND ALSO,
that the said part   of the second part,   executors,
administrators or assigns, or any of them, shall not, nor
will, at any time hereafter, during the term hereby granted,
erect, make, establish or carry on, nor cause or suffer to be
erected, made, established or carried on, in any manner, on
any part of the above described and hereby demised premises, any stable, slaughter house, tallow chandlery, smith
shop, forge, furnace, or brass foundry, nail or other iron
factory, or any manufactory for the making of glass, starch,
glue, varnish, vitriol, turpentine or ink ; or for tanning,
dressing, preparing or keeping skins, hides or leather ; or
any distillery, brewery, sugar bakery, or any other manufactory, trade, business or calling whatsoever, which may
be in anywise noxious or offensive to the neighboring
inhabitants. AND LASTLY, that the said part   of the
second part,   executors, administrators or assigns,
shall and will, on the last day of the term hereby granted,
or other sooner determination thereof, well and truly sur-

render and deliver up the said hereby demised premises into the possession of the said parties of the first part, their successors or assigns, without fraud or delay. PROVIDED ALWAYS, that it shall be lawful for the said parties of the first part, their successors and assigns, when and as often as default shall be made in the payment of the said rent, or any part thereof, to take such summary proceedings for the recovery of the said rent as may be permitted by law, anything herein contained to the contrary notwithstanding. AND PROVIDED FURTHER, and this present lease is upon this express condition. That if the said part   of the second part,   executors, administrators or assigns, shall at any time during the term hereby granted, erect, make, establish or carry on, or cause, or suffer to be erected, made, established or carried on, in any manner, on any part of the above described and hereby demised premises, any stable, slaughter house, tallow chandlery, smith shop, forge, furnace or brass foundry, nail or other iron factory, or any manufactory for the making of glass, starch, glue, varnish, vitriol, turpentine or ink ; or for tanning, dressing, preparing or keeping skins, hides or leather ; or any distillery, brewery, sugar bakery, or any other manufactory, trade, business or calling whatsoever, which may be in anywise noxious or offensive to the neighboring inhabitants, or shall fail in the performance of any or either of the covenants, conditions or provisoes in these presents contained, which on the part and behalf of the said part   of the second part,   executors, administrators and assigns, are, or ought to be, observed, performed, fulfilled and kept, then and from thenceforth, this present indenture and the estate hereby granted, and every clause, article and thing herein contained, on the part and behalf of the said parties of the first part, to be performed, fulfilled and kept, shall cease, determine, and be utterly void, to all intents and purposes whatsoever, anything herein contained to the contrary thereof in anywise notwithstanding.

AND it is hereby mutually covenanted and agreed, that at the expiration of the term hereby granted, if the said parties hereto shall agree upon a renewal of this lease, for a further term of twenty-one years, and shall, by mutual consent, fix upon the annual ground rent to be reserved in such renewed lease, then the said parties of the first part, their successors or assigns, shall and will execute to the said part of the second part, executors, administrators or assigns, at their expense, a new lease of the aforesaid premises for the term of twenty-one years, from and after the expiration of the term hereby granted, at the annual ground rent, payable half-yearly, agreed upon between the said parties as aforesaid. But if, at the expiration of the term hereby granted, the said parties shall not agree upon a renewal of this lease, or upon the amount of the rent to be reserved for such renewed term, then each party shall choose a disinterested person, who shall be the owner in fee simple of one or more lots of land in the neighborhood of the premises hereby demised, and the said persons so chosen shall, under oath, appraise the land hereby demised, considering it as a vacant lot, at its full and fair worth at private sale ; and they shall also, under oath, appraise the building now erected on the said lot, or any other building of like description as its substitute—which shall cover the whole front of such lot, be constructed of brick or stone, or more stories high, and covered with slate or metal, with its front finished in such style as may be approved of by the said parties of the first part, their successors or assigns—at its then actual worth, without reference to the ground on which it stands ; and in case the said appraisers shall differ in their valuation or appraisement, either of the lot or building, they shall then choose an umpire, qualified as aforesaid, whose decision, under oath, shall be final and conclusive.

AND the said parties of the first part, their successors or assigns, shall have the full liberty and choice, either to pay to the said part of the second part, executors, administrators or assigns, the value of the said building so determined as aforesaid, or to grant a renewal of this lease unto the said part of the second part, executors, administrators or assigns, at their expense, for the term of twenty-one years from and after the expiration of the term hereby granted, at an annual ground rent of five per cent. on the valuation of the said lot so determined as aforesaid.

AND it is further mutually covenanted and agreed, that at the expiration of each and every term which may be thereafter granted by each and every subsequent renewal of this lease, the said parties of the first part, their successors or assigns, shall still have and retain the full liberty and choice, either to grant a further renewal, for the further term of twenty-one years, at such annual rent, payable half-yearly, as shall be ascertained and determined in the manner aforesaid, or to pay unto the said part of the second part, executors, administrators or assigns, the value of the said building or its substitute, to be ascertained as aforesaid. And it is further mutually covenanted and agreed, by and between the parties aforesaid, that whenever the said parties of the first part, their successors or assigns, shall refuse to grant a renewal of this lease, as aforesaid, the said building or its substitute shall be valued and paid for as aforesaid. PROVIDED ALWAYS, that the said part of the second part, executors, administrators or assigns, shall not be compelled to surrender the premises until such payment be made or tendered. And it is further mutually covenanted and agreed, by and between the parties aforesaid, that in case the said parties of the first part, their successors or assigns, shall, at the expiration of the term granted by this lease, or at the expiration of any term which may be granted thereafter by any subsequent renewal thereof, elect and choose to pay unto the said part of the second part, executors, administrators or assigns, the value of the said building or its substitute, to be ascertained as aforesaid, and shall actually make such payment, or tender the same, the said part of the second part, executors, administrators or assigns, shall then deliver up the said building or its substitute, in the same order and condition in which it was at the time of its valuation, as aforesaid, and also all and singular other the premises hereby demised, to the said parties of the first part, their successors or assigns, without fraud or delay. AND LASTLY, it is mutually covenanted and agreed, by and between the parties aforesaid, that each renewed lease shall contain the like covenants, provisoes and conditions as herein contained.

In Witness whereof, the said parties of the first part have caused their corporate seal to be hereunto affixed ; and the said part of the second part ha set hand and seal interchangeably, the day and year first above written.

STATE OF NEW YORK, } ss.:
City and County of New York, }

On the day of A. D. one thousand eight hundred and before me personally appeared
'

to me known, who, being by me duly sworn, did state that he is the of the Trustees of the SAILORS' SNUG HARBOR in the city of New York, the Corporation described in, and which executed the foregoing Indenture of Lease ; that he resides in the said city ; that the seal affixed to the said Indenture of Lease is the Corporate Seal of the said The Trustees of the SAILORS' SNUG HARBOR in the city of New York, and was affixed thereto by their authority.

The following is a copy of the By-Laws and of the Rules by which the Sailors' Snug Harbor is governed, viz.:

BY-LAWS

OF THE

Sailors' Snug Harbor,

PUBLISHED BY ORDER OF THE TRUSTEES.

———— •◦• ————

NEW YORK:
SLOTE & JANES, STATIONERS AND PRINTERS, 93 FULTON STREET.
1876.

SAILORS' SNUG HARBOR.

PREAMBLE.

By the last will and testament of the late Captain ROBERT RICHARD RANDALL, certain property was bequeathed " to erect and build an Asylum or Marine Hospital, to be called the ' Sailors' Snug Harbor,' for the purpose of maintaining and supporting aged, decrepit and worn-out Sailors." In pursuance of the provisions of said will, and of the Act of Incorporation afterwards obtained, the administration of the trust so created is now committed to the following persons, *ex officio*, viz.:

The Mayor of the City of New York,

The Recorder of the City of New York,

The President of the Chamber of Commerce of the City of New York,

The President of the Marine Society of the City of New York.

The First Vice-President of the Marine Society of the City of New York,

The Rector of Trinity Church, of the City of New York, and

The Minister of the First Presbyterian Church, of the City of New York,

who, with their successors in office, constitute a body corporate under the name and style of " THE TRUSTEES OF THE SAILORS' SNUG HARBOR IN THE CITY OF NEW YORK." Said corporation, by virtue of the powers so committed to them, do hereby ordain and establish the following

BY-LAWS.

ARTICLE I.

OF THE OFFICE OF THE TRUSTEES.

There shall be established and kept in the City of New York a suitable place for the transaction of business, which shall be designated, " Office of the Trustees of the Sailors' Snug Harbor."

ARTICLE II.

OF MEETINGS OF THE TRUSTEES.

Stated Meetings of the Trustees shall be held at their office, or elsewhere as may be appointed, during the months of March, June, September and December in each year. Special Meetings may also be convened and held at the call of the President. Five members shall constitute a quorum.*

ARTICLE III.

OF OFFICERS OF THE BOARD.

SECTION 1.—The Officers of the Board shall be a President, who must be one of the Trustees, a Controller, and a Secretary, who shall be elected annually by ballot, at the stated meeting in March, and shall hold their offices during the pleasure of the Board. Vacancies may be filled at any meeting.

---

* Act of Incorporation, Sec. 2.

SEC. 2.—The Controller, and such other officers as shall, in the discharge of their duties, be intrusted with the custody of money or other property of the Corporation, "shall give such security for the faithful execution of their duty, and the performance of the trusts reposed in them respectively," * as is hereinafter or otherwise designated.

OF THE PRESIDENT.

SEC. 3.—The President shall have custody of the official bonds given by the Controller and other officers. He shall preside at all meetings of the Board, and sign all leases, contracts, and other documents authorized by them. In his absence from any meeting of the Board, a Chairman shall be chosen to preside in his stead.

OF THE CONTROLLER.

SEC. 4.—The Controller shall give security by a bond, satisfactory to the Board, in the sum of fifteen thousand dollars, for the faithful performance of his duties.

SEC. 5.—He shall, under the direction of the Board, have immediate charge of the Office of the Trustees, and of all funds, records, books, leases, securities and documents, and the supervision of all persons employed therein.

SEC. 6.—He shall collect all dues accruing to the Corporation, whether from rents, interest or otherwise, and give proper receipts for the same. He shall take care that all covenants and undertakings of lessees of property of the Corporation are duly complied with, and in case of any default or failure therein, to notify forthwith the Executive Committee.

SEC. 7.—He shall keep regular books of account, in which shall be entered all receipts and payments by or for

*Act of Incorporation, Sec. 2.

the Trustees, and which shall at all times exhibit the state of the finances of the Corporation.

SEC. 8.—All moneys belonging to the Corporation shall be deposited to the credit of the Trustees, in such bank or other moneyed institution as may be designated by the Board. No part thereof shall be drawn unless by appropriation previously made by the Board or Executive Committee, and then only by the check of the Controller to the order of the party to receive the amount. All checks shall be countersigned by the Chairman of the Executive Committee, or some other member thereof. In case of the absence or inability of the Controller, such checks may be signed by the President or a member of the Executive Committee.

SEC. 9.—In order that the funds of the Corporation may be improved to the best advantage, it shall be the duty of the Controller to exhibit to the Executive Committee, at least once a month, and oftener when requested, a statement of the receipts, payments, and balances on deposit in bank, with the sums to be received and paid out during the ensuing month. He shall also report to the Board at each stated meeting, the amount of the receipts and payments since the last previous meeting, with the balance then in bank, also an estimate of the moneys to be received and payments to be made before another meeting.

SEC. 10.—All requisitions for supplies for the Institution shall be made, through the Governor, to the Controller, and by him submitted to the Executive Committee. If approved by said Committee, they shall be filled by the Controller by purchase on the best terms practicable. All purchases shall be made for net cash, payable within thirty days. Separate invoices, in duplicate, shall be taken for articles bought for the different departments, which shall be transmitted to the Governor, with the goods, for examination, and subsequently be returned by him to the Controller. But no such bills shall be paid until they are duly certified by the Steward, Physician, Superintendent, Engineer, Matron, or other Head of Department for which such purchase was made, and also approved by the Governor.

Sec. 11.—The certification of bills by the heads of the departments using the articles specified therein, as required by the preceding section, shall be in these words: "The above articles received, examined and found correct;" and shall be signed by the proper official. Such certificate shall be deemed and held to signify that the officer signing the same personally examined the articles and found the kinds, quantities, and qualities thereof as specified. The approval of the Governor shall be expressed by the word "Approved," in writing, to which his signature shall be affixed; and the same shall be held to declare and signify that the articles specified in said bill were necessary and proper to be procured, and that the kinds, quantities and qualities thereof actually received were as specified therein. If the Controller find any error or discrepancy therein, he shall at once return said bills to the Governor for correction.

Sec. 12.—The Controller shall designate one or more days in each month when he will personally attend at the Governor's office, in the Institution, prepared to settle all local bills, including the wages of laborers and others employed in and about the Institution.

Sec. 13.—All bills and pay-rolls, when paid, shall be duly receipted, and thereupon properly indorsed and filed by the Controller in the office of the Trustees, the duplicate to be returned to the Governor.

Sec. 14.—The Controller shall prepare the annual reports required by law to be made by the Corporation to the Legislature of the State of New York, and to the Common Council of the City of New York, subject to the approval of the Board.

Sec. 15.—All papers, documents and books kept by the Governor, or other officers of the Institution, shall at all times be open to the inspection of the Trustees and the Controller, who shall also have the right to require from any official or other person in the service of the Board, such statements or information concerning the affairs of the Institution as they may desire, which information shall be promptly given. All instructions in relation to the time and manner of performing their ordinary duties shall be communicated and given through the Governor, who shall be held answerable therefor.

Sec. 16.—The Controller shall attend the meetings of the Trustees, for the purpose of giving them information concerning the affairs of the Corporation, and receiving their instructions in relation to the duties to be performed by him.

OF THE SECRETARY.

Sec. 17.—The Secretary shall give due notice of all meetings of the Board and of the Standing Committees. He shall attend all such meetings and keep accurate minutes of their proceedings, which shall always be authenticated by his signature. He shall keep the Corporation Seal, and affix the same to any documents when directed by the Board, and shall also sign the leases and transfers of same made by the Board.

ARTICLE IV.

OF THE EXECUTIVE COMMITTEE.

Section 1.—There shall be appointed annually, at the stated meeting in March, an Executive Committee, consisting of three Trustees; two members shall be a quorum. The minutes of their proceedings shall be read and submitted to the approval of the Board at its next regular meeting. Special Committees may be appointed at any time, as occasion shall require.

Sec. 2.—It shall be the duty of the Executive Committee to carry into effect the orders of the Board, and act for them provisionally, in the intervals between their meetings, in matters which have not already been referred to some other Committee, or otherwise disposed of.

Sec. 3.—Said Committee shall counsel and direct the Controller, as far as they shall deem necessary, in the care and management of the funds and other property of the Corporation, and as to the purchase of the supplies needed for the Institution, or for the office of the Trustees. All instructions to the Governor of the Institution by said Committee, or by the Board of Trustees, shall be in writing, communicated to him by the Controller.

Sec. 4.—In case of unexpected emergencies, the Executive Committee may, at their discretion, either call a special meeting of the Board, or themselves authorize a sufficient appropriation of money to meet such emergencies.

Sec. 5.—The Executive Committee shall be authorized to issue certificates approving of buildings to be erected and improvements to be made on the leased property of this Corporation, provided said Committee is satisfied that the rights of the Trustees are in no wise impaired by such buildings or improvements. The following shall be the form of the certificate, viz. :

" The Executive Committee of the Trustees of the Sailors' Snug Harbor, by virtue of the authority vested in them by Sec. 5, Article IV. of the By-Laws of said Corporation, do hereby certify that we have examined the buildings and improvements on Lot No.   , on map of their property in the 15th Ward of the City of New York, and that they are in conformity with the terms of the lease."

Sec. 6.—It shall be the duty of said Committee to see that all real estate owned by the Corporation, and not re-

quired for the actual occupation of the Trustees, is duly
rented on the most advantageous terms.

SEC. 7.—It shall also be the duty of said Committee,
under the direction of the Board, to superintend all loans
or investments made or to be made from time to time, and
to see that all interest, rents and other dues to be received
are regularly collected.

SEC. 8.—The vouchers taken for payments made, and the
accounts kept by the Controller, shall, as often as once in
every six months, be carefully examined and audited by
the Executive Committee. All securities and moneys belonging to the Corporation, whether in the custody of the
Controller or on deposit in bank, shall also be examined in
like manner.

ARTICLE V.

OF THE INSTITUTION AND ITS MANAGEMENT.

SECTION 1.—The administration of the Institution on
Staten Island shall, under the direction of the Board of
Trustees, be committed to a Governor, a Chaplain, a Physician, an Agent, and a Steward. All these persons shall
be elected, and shall hold their offices and receive their sal-
aries, subject to the following conditions and restrictions

They shall be assisted in the administration by the following subordinates, viz.: a farmer, an engineer, a matron,
and others, all of whom shall be appointed or authorized
by the Board of Trustees, upon nomination of the Governor.
All the persons designated in this section, except the Agent,
shall reside at the Institution, and shall perform the duties
hereinafter specified, and such others as may reasonably be
required of them by the Governor, or by the Board.

OF THE GOVERNOR.

SEC. 2.—The Governor shall, under the direction of the
Trustees, have immediate charge, supervision, and control

of the Institution and farm on Staten Island; also, of all officers and servants employed there, and of the inmates admitted to the privileges of the same, and shall devote the whole of his time and attention to the discharge of his official duties. He shall give security by a bond for five thousand dollars for the faithful performance of said duties.

SEC. 3.—He shall, in addition to his stated salary, be allowed the use of the mansion and garden appropriated for the official residence and occupation of the Governor, which residence, with the fences surrounding the garden, shall be kept in good tenantable repair at the expense of this Corporation.

SEC. 4.—All orders of the Trustees, or of any Committee, relating to the Institution, or to the administration of its affairs, shall be in writing, addressed to the Governor, and transmitted by the Controller.

SEC. 5.—If any of the administrative officers named in the first section of this Article shall neglect to comply with the lawful requirements of the Governor, or fail to perform any part of his official duty, the Governor may reprimand such person at his discretion, and in case of similar neglect by any of the subordinates specified in the same section, the Governor may both reprimand and suspend such offender; in all cases reporting such action forthwith to the Board of Trustees, with his reasons therefor.

SEC. 6.—It shall be his duty to reprimand, and if the offense be repeated, to suspend from the privileges of the Institution, any inmate who shall wilfully transgress the regulations thereof; and such inmate, while under suspension, shall be forbidden to remain upon the premises, and if, notwithstanding, he persist in so doing, it shall be the duty of the Governor to cause him to be arrested for trespass, or otherwise lawfully removed. He shall immediately report every such case of suspension to the Executive Committee, and present to the Trustees, at their next regular meeting, a copy of the record of the suspended person, who shall, at the same time, be permitted to state his own case, and the Trustees shall thereupon, by vote, reinstate said person, suspend him for a limited term, or permanently expel him. Any inmate so expelled shall not be re-admitted except by the vote of the Board.

Sec. 7.—In case any person who has been admitted as an inmate of the Institution shall become restored to health, so as to be able to earn his own living, or shall in any other way acquire the means of supporting himself, it shall be the duty of the Governor and Physician to report the fact to the Executive Committee, to the end that they may take such order in the case as may be required by a faithful discharge of the trust.

Sec. 8.—It shall be the duty of the Governor to see that all assessments levied on the property of the Corporation on Staten Island for taxes or local improvements, are not excessive in amount, or out of due proportion to the like assessments on other property in the same town or neighborhood.

Sec. 9.—It shall be the duty of the Governor to cause requisitions to be made monthly, or oftener if necessary, by the heads of the several departments of the Institution, for all articles and supplies required by them. If such requisitions are approved by him, he shall endorse them to that effect, with the date, and a copy thereof shall be entered in a book kept in his office labelled "Requisitions." He shall then transmit them to the Controller, with any needful explanations as to their use and necessity. Upon receiving the invoices for said articles, the Governor shall deliver them to the proper heads of departments for examination, and if found correct, they shall be so certified and returned to the Governor.

SEC. 10.—It shall be his duty to inspect all articles received, and see that they correspond to the requisitions and invoices, and if found correct, to indorse said invoices duly certified as aforesaid with his approval, and transmit them monthly to the Controller for settlement; the same to be regularly numbered and accompanied by a schedule thereof; when paid, the duplicates to be returned by the Controller to the Governor, who shall then copy them at length in a book to be kept in his office, labeled " Invoice Book."

SEC. 11.—All bills for repairs and improvements upon buildings, fences, furniture, tools, etc., including materials used, shall in like manner, if found correct, be certified by the Head of the proper Department and approved by the Governor. All such bills shall be copied into a book to be kept in his office, labeled " Repairs and Improvements," and thereupon transmitted to the Controller for settlement, monthly, *provided*, however, that no bills shall be incurred (except in case of pressing urgency) unless the same shall have been previously authorized by the Board of Trustees or the Executive Committee, and a suitable appropriation made to cover the expense thereof. All such bills shall have indorsed upon them, in red ink, the date of the resolution of the Board or Executive Committee by which the same was authorized.

SEC. 12.—It shall be the duty of the Governor to preserve in a book to be kept in his office, labeled " Instructions," and properly indexed, all resolutions of the Board of Trustees, or of the Executive Committee, relative to his office or duties, and all communications from the Controller.

SEC. 13.—The Governor shall require quarterly reports from the heads of the several Departments of the nature and extent of the service or work performed, and all noteworthy occurrences in said Departments during the quarter.

SEC. 14.—It shall be the duty of the Governor to make

frequent visits to all the buildings and grounds, and to
inspect the rooms, stores, crops, stock, etc., to the end that
he may be fully and reliably informed respecting every de-
tail of the administration of the Institution, and be thereby
enabled to give such directions as shall promote order and
economy in all expenditures, and secure the greatest comfort to the inmates.

Sec. 15.—The Governor shall appoint and give due notice of the hours when he will be in his office, prepared to
receive applications for permits, and to hear and determine
all complaints.

Sec. 16.—He shall take care to have the grounds, roads
and walks within the inclosure kept in good order, and the
trees and shrubbery properly pruned, which work, it is expected, will generally be done by the inmates.

Sec. 17.—The Governor will be expected to attend divine service in the chapel on Sundays. He shall designate
a suitable person among the inmates to ring the chapel bell,
and shall be expected, unless other duties forbid, to be
present at the burial of deceased inmates.

Sec. 18.—He shall take care that all the produce from
the farm and garden is properly gathered, also that all
grease and other refuse from the kitchen, and all old iron,
lead, copper, rags, boxes, barrels and other like articles,
are carefully collected, and disposed of at such times and in
such manner as may be directed by the Controller. All
moneys arising from the sale of such articles shall, without
any deduction or reservation, be paid into the treasury of
the Corporation. He shall enter in a suitable book, to be
kept in his office, labeled "Sales Book," an account of all
such articles, giving names of purchasers, dates, and the
amounts realized thereby.

Sec. 19.—The Governor may authorize the delivery to

officers and employees (and to no others) of coal and bread, at the actual cost to the Institution, including freight and expenses. Such articles shall be duly entered in the ".Sales Book," above mentioned, and detailed monthly accounts of the same rendered to the Controller, and settled at the end of the month.

SEC. 20.—He shall report to the Controller whenever there is any surplus or excess in the supply of stores, produce, materials or live stock on hand, beyond what may be wanted, with his suggestions as to the best disposition to be made of the same.

SEC. 21.—The .Governor may appoint from among the inmates of the Institution, one or more Inspectors, whose duty it shall be to report to him all irregularities of conduct or disobedience of orders among the inmates, and to give their aid and co-operation in carrying into effect the rules prescribed by the Trustees. He may also designate inmates to perform the duties of lodge-keepers. The inspectors and lodge-keepers shall have separate tables and apartments, and hold their offices during the pleasure of the Governor, who shall report their names to the Board quarterly. He may, when necessary, authorize the heads of departments to employ temporary assistance beyond what may reasonably be required of the inmates.

SEC. 22.—The Governor shall enter in a Register to be kept in his office, as per printed form of said Register, a record of every inmate. He shall also keep a register of persons visiting the Institution, the names of whom shall be reported to him daily by the lodge-keepers. No visitors will be allowed on Sundays without special permission from the Governor or Physician.

SEC. 23.—He shall also keep a record of the names of officers of the Corporation, and other visitors entitled by usage to be treated with hospitality, who may be entertained at his house as guests of the Institution ; a monthly report of whom shall be rendered to the Controller, in order that due provision may be made by the Trustees for reimbursing the expense of such entertainments.

SEC. 24.—The Governor shall make a quarterly report to the Trustees, stating the whole number of inmates at the date of the last previous report, their increase by admissions, their decrease by expulsion, discharge and death, the number remaining and the number absent on liberty. This report shall also contain a general account of the expenses of the Institution for the quarter, and the average cost per diem of the maintenance of the inmates; together with a general resumè of all matters pertaining to the Institution and its inmates, and any suggestions which he shall deem useful for the information and guidance of the Trustees for im_ proving the general administration of the trust and promoting the welfare of its beneficiaries. In keeping the accounts and estimating the expenses of the Institution, all the produce of the farm and garden shall be appraised and reckoned at its current market value. The price of bread and other articles from the bakery shall be reckoned at the cost of flour, including freight and cartage.

SEC. 25.—In case of sickness, absence or inability on the part of the Governor, the Physician, with the concurrence of the Controller, shall have authority to act in his stead, until other provision shall be made.

OF THE CHAPLAIN.

SEC. 26.—The Chaplain, under direction of the Governor, shall have the moral and spiritual oversight of the Institution, and of all persons, whether officers, servants, or bene ficiaries, residing therein, and shall devote his whole time and attention to the discharge of his duties.

Sec. 27.—He shall, in addition to his stated salary, be allowed the use of the dwelling-house and garden appropriated for the residence of said officer. Said residence with the fences surrounding the garden, shall be maintained and kept in good, tenantable repair, at the expense of this Corporation.

Sec. 28.—He shall hold divine service every Sunday, in the chapel, both in the morning and in the afternoon, and conduct the usual daily religious exercises, morning and evening, in the central building, in the room appropriated for that purpose, except at such other times as may be appointed in the hall of the hospital.

Sec. 29.—He shall minister at the bedside of the sick and afflicted, and at the burial of the dead, and perform all such offices and duties as usually and properly devolve upon the ministers of Christ in the strictest fulfillment of their vocation.

Sec. 30.—In case of absence on leave, sickness or other disability of the Chaplain, he shall be authorized, with the approval of the Governor, to invite another clergyman or suitable person to conduct the stated religious services, for which compensation shall be paid by the Corporation. All bills for such services shall be certified by the Chaplain, and if considered correct, be approved by the Governor.

Sec. 31.—All officers, employees and inmates of the Institution shall be expected to attend public worship in the chapel every Sunday, unless prevented by sickness or other sufficient cause.

Sec. 32.—Any officer, employee or inmate who is a member of any church of a different denomination from that of the Chaplain, if he shall desire to attend divine service, statedly or occasionally, elsewhere than at the chapel of the Institution, shall be permitted to do so, on presenting to the Governor his request in writing to that effect, stating the place, and indorsed by the officiating minister at such place. Any inmate who shall abuse the privilege thus granted, shall forfeit his right to a similar favor thereafter.

SEC. 33.—The Chaplain, with the approval of the Governor, may appoint an organist for the chapel, who shall receive from the Board such compensation as they may deem proper.

SEC. 34.—The Chaplain shall have supervision of the library and reading-room, and with the approval of the Governor may designate not exceeding five daily and seven weekly newspapers and three monthly periodicals, to be supplied to the reading-room for the use of the officers and inmates. It shall be his duty summarily to exclude from the premises any publication or print, of whatever kind, of any immoral or improper character.

SEC 35.—He may, with the approval of the Governor, appoint a suitable person from among the inmates to act as Librarian and Superintendent of the reading-room, whose duty it shall be to keep the books and papers in order, and see that the prescribed regulations for the use thereof are observed.

SEC. 36.—It shall be the duty of the Chaplain to make a quarterly report to the Governor for the information of the Trustees, respecting the moral and religious state of the people of his charge, and to offer such suggestions therein for the improvement of their condition as he may deem useful; said report shall also state the services performed by him, and in cases of his absence the dates thereof, with names and residences of clergymen officiating in his stead.

SEC. 37.—Sundays and all legal holidays shall be duly observed by all persons connected with the Institution, and no visitors shall be allowed admission within the inclosure on those days without permission from the Governor or Physician.

Sec. 38.—It shall be the duty of all the inmates of the Institution to appear on Sunday clean and neatly clad, and to maintain the quiet and orderly deportment becoming the sanctity of the Lord's day. In case of any violation of this rule, or of any breach of good morals by the use of profane or impure language, or otherwise, it shall be the Chaplain's duty to administer suitable reproof therefor, and if the offence be repeated, to report the same to the Governor for discipline.

OF THE PHYSICIAN.

Sec. 39.—The Physician shall, under the direction of the Governor, have entire charge of the sanitary regulations of the Institution. He shall devote his whole time and attention to the care of the sick and infirm, whether officers, servants or inmates, and prescribe such rules of hygiene as may be necessary for the preservation of health.

Sec. 40.—In addition to his stated salary, he shall be allowed the use of the dwelling and garden appropriated for said officer. Said residence, with the fences surrounding the garden, shall be maintained and kept in good tenantable repair, at the expense of the Corporation.

Sec. 41.—It shall be his duty to keep a record of every case requiring his professional attention, and of the remedies and treatment prescribed by him.

Sec. 42.—He shall make requisitions in writing monthly, or oftener, through the Governor, for all needful medicines and stores, and shall have the care and dispensing thereof. He shall notify the Governor, in writing, whenever any repairs are necessary to the hospital or its furniture, or any renewals of the same.

SEC. 43.—He shall, under the Governor, have exclusive charge and control, both of the hospital and of its inmates, whether servants or patients, and shall report to the Governor any neglect of duty, disrespectful behavior, or other misconduct on the part of those under his supervision.

SEC. 44.—He shall report to the Governor, in writing, the name of any inmate whom he shall believe to be insane, or whose continuance at large and without restraint he shall consider unsafe.

SEC. 45.—He shall examine every person who may be temporarily admitted into the Institution, and report to the Governor in writing, his condition, and especially whether he is afflicted with any contagious disease. Said report shall be transmitted to the Trustees for their consideration, before such person shall be admitted to full membership of the Institution.

SEC. 46.—It shall be the duty of the Physician to expel from the Hospital any inmate who shall disobey his orders, or who does not conform to the rules and regulations of the Hospital. No inmate in the Hospital shall be allowed to go outside the inclosure without a permit, in writing, from the Physician.

SEC. 47.—He shall examine the condition of any inmate who may claim exemption from work on the ground of illness or disability, and give a certificate of his opinion of the case for presentation to the Governor.

SEC. 48.—He shall be authorized, with the concurrence of the Governor, to appoint a head nurse and such number of assistant nurses and cooks for the Hospital as he may deem necessary, and prescribe their duties. Their compensation shall be determined by the Executive Committee.

SEC. 49.—Upon the death of any inmate, the Physician shall report to the Governor his name and cause of death, with such particulars as will be of interest to surviving friends; a copy of which shall be transmitted to the Agent for record.

SEC. 50.—He shall order the daily diet for the inmates of the Hospital, and keep a correct account of all supplies received for the use of the Hospital.

SEC. 51.—He shall also render a quarterly report to the Governor for the information of the Trustees as to the general sanitary condition of the Institution, stating the number of deaths during the quarter, the number of sick and infirm patients, and the general character of their diseases, with any suggestions concerning the Hospital which he may deem useful; also the condition of the insane.

SEC. 52.—The Physician shall be authorized, with the sanction of the Governor, to consult other physicians and surgeons in cases of unusual importance. In case of his sickness or necessary absence, the Governor may secure other medical attendance. In all such cases, the Resident Physician shall report to the Governor the proper compensation to be allowed, in order that the bills may be audited and settled monthly.

SEC. 53.—He shall visit the insane inmates yearly, and report their condition to the Trustees.

OF THE AGENT.

SEC. 54.—The Agent shall be provided with suitable accommodations in the office of the Trustees, in the City of New York, and shall devote the whole of his time and attention to the service of the Corporation.

SEC. 55.—It shall be the duty of the Agent to furnish persons who may contemplate making application for admission to the privileges of the Institution, with a copy of so much of these By-Laws and Regulations as relates to the duties of the inmates, and with such additional information as may be necessary.

SEC. 56.—It shall also be the duty of the Agent to see that the following regulations as to admissions are fully complied with :

Every application for admission must be made out in duplicate on the printed blank prescribed for the purpose—full and explicit answers being required to all of the interrogatories contained therein, the agent being empowered at his discretion to require said answers to be given under oath. They must also state that the applicant has promised a strict and willing compliance with the laws of the Institution. Such application must be accompanied by testimonials showing that the applicant has been a sailor, that he is without adequate means of support, and is possessed of all the requisite qualifications for admission, which must be therein set forth.*

SEC. 57.—All such applications, with the accompanying testimonials, shall be referred to the Agent for examination, and it shall be his duty by questioning the applicants, and correspondence with and personal inquiries of the parties referred to by applicants, and any others, to ascertain and determine in regard to the eligibility of such persons to admission. If, after making such examination and inquiries, he shall deem such applicant eligible to temporary admission, he shall date and sign the Agent's certificate of approval printed on the application. If such application shall be also approved and endorsed by not less than two Trustees, the applicant, on presenting his application so approved and endorsed to the Governor, with a list of his clothing subscribed by him, will be entitled to temporary admission into the Institution. In case of doubt as to any applicant, he shall at once refer the case to the Executive Committee for their decision.

---

* The qualifications requisite for admission are set forth on page 34.

SEC. 58.—It shall be the duty of the Agent to record in a book to be kept by him, to be labeled "Applications for Admission," the number, name, place and date of birth, and the nature and time of service as a sailor, of every applicant, with the names and addresses of his references, and an account of the information received from them respectively, together with an abstract of applicant's written testimonials, and also the disposition made of the case.

SEC. 59.—The Agent shall also keep, in a book to be provided for the purpose, to be labeled "Records of Inmates," the name of every inmate, with a succinct history of his life and conduct while a member of the Institution, as reported by the Governor.

SEC. 60.—In addition to the foregoing, it shall be the duty of the Agent to assist the Controller in the performance of his duties, as may be required by him.

OF THE STEWARD.

SEC. 61.—The Steward shall give a bond, satisfactory to the Board, for five thousand dollars for the faithful performance of his duties.

SEC. 62.—He shall, under the direction of the Governor, be the storekeeper of the Institution, and shall have charge of all groceries, provisions, clothing, and other articles for the use of the inmates, and shall superintend the receipt and delivery of the same.

SEC. 63.—In addition to his stated salary, he shall be allowed the use of the dwelling-house appropriated for said officer, which shall be kept in repair by the Institution, and a plot of ground for a garden.

SEC. 64.—Before registering any person as a temporary inmate, the Steward shall see that his clothing corresponds with the list thereof furnished by him, which list shall be copied into a Clothes Book to be kept in the Steward's office.

SEC. 65.—If any person registered, either as a temporary or permanent inmate, shall be discharged or leave on liberty, his name shall be recorded by the Steward and his rations stopped.

SEC. 66.—Clothing will be furnished to the inmates and kept in repair, but no new article shall be supplied without a written order from the Governor, to be filed in the Steward's office, and the delivery of the old garments for which the new was substituted. All cast-off clothing shall be preserved and disposed of as ordered by the Controller.

SEC. 67.—He shall, under the Governor, have charge of the dining-halls, kitchen, bakery and dormitories, and the supervision of all persons employed in them. The Governor shall, at his request, designate suitable persons among the inmates to assist him in the performance of his duties.

SEC. 68.—He shall make out the daily requisitions for provisions, specifying the kinds and quantities of meat, fish, bread and other articles required, which requisitions, signed by the Governor, he shall keep on file in his office. He shall also, with the Governor's approval, direct what articles shall be prepared and served at each meal, and shall remain in the dining-rooms during meals to preserve order and prevent waste.

SEC. 69.—He shall examine all supplies received for the use of his department, and certify the invoices thereof, if correct, as required in Section 11 of Article III. He shall enter a list of all supplies received in a book, labeled "Daily Receipts."

SEC. 70.—He shall keep Pass Books with the butcher, baker, gardener and farmer, in which shall be entered daily the kinds, quantities and value of articles received from each. Such Pass Books shall be footed monthly, and the aggregate of each be entered in the Daily Receipt Book mentioned in the last section, and reported to the Governor.

SEC. 71.—He shall also keep a Pass Book with the shoemaker, for work ordered for the inmates, to be entered therein monthly, with the prices, the aggregate amount at the end of each month to be stated therein, entered in the Daily Receipt Book, and reported to the Governor.

SEC. 72.—He shall keep an account of the time of mechanics and laborers employed by the day in his department, and of the materials used, and certify the same to the Governor in the prescribed forms for pay-rolls and other accounts.

SEC. 73.—He shall keep exact accounts of all supplies for inmates, delivered to the cooks and others upon the daily or other requisitions of the Governor and Physician ; also of all bread and coal sold to the officers and employees of the Institution, including his own family ; and shall furnish transcripts of such accounts monthly to the Governor.

SEC. 74.—The Steward shall take care that the clock in the main hall is regularly wound up and kept in time, and that the ringing of the bell for all occasions, as appointed by the Governor, is duly attended to.

SEC. 75.—He shall keep his store-rooms and cellars clean and in order, have all barrels and firkins cleansed, their heads replaced and re-hooped so as to be available for use or sale to the best advantage. He shall carefully inspect the fresh beef, mutton and fowls delivered to the Harbor, and if they are not of proper quality and perfectly fresh, report the fact immediately to the Governor.

SEC. 76.—He shall take care to have the grease arising

from the cooking of meats in the kitchen carefully collected
and taken care of until disposed of.

Sec. 77.—He shall superintend the lodges at the gates
and the keepers of them (who shall be designated from
among the inmates by or with the approval of the Governor),
and take care that the regulations prescribed by the By-
Laws respecting the entrance and departure of persons and
parcels through the gates are strictly enforced.

Sec. 78.—He shall on the death of an inmate take an
inventory of his effects, to be signed by him and delivered
to the Governor. The clothing and other articles furnished
by the Institution shall be retained and put under the care
of the Matron. All personal effects of deceased inmates shall
be taken care of by the Governor, and disposed of as may
be directed by the Trustees.

Sec. 79.—He shall give all necessary orders for the burial
of the dead, and be present at all interments in the Cemetery of the Institution, and make a record of the location of
the grave.

Sec. 80.—He shall, once a quarter, take an inventory of
stores on hand in his department and report the same to the
Governor, stating the total quantities of all articles received,
consumed by inmates, and furnished to officers and employees during the previous quarter.

Sec. 81.—He shall report to the Governor the names of
all inmates leaving the Institution without permission, and
all instances of drunkenness, swearing, obscenity, insub-
ordination, infractions or neglect of the rules and regulations
taking place within his knowledge.

Sec. 82.—In case of a vacancy occurring in the office of
Steward, the Governor, with the concurrence of the Controller, shall be authorized to make a temporary appointment

to fill the same. In case of sickness or absence of the Steward, provision shall be made in the same manner for the continued discharge of his duties.

OF THE SUBORDINATE OFFICERS.

Sec. 83.—All the subordinate officers mentioned in Section 1 of this Article shall, in addition to their ordinary duties, perform such other reasonable services as the Governor may from time to time require, and shall not be absent from the Institution without his consent. The Governor has power to make such rules and regulations as he may deem proper for the management of the different departments of the Institution; such rules, when approved by the Executive Committee, shall be obeyed by the officers, employees and inmates.

Sec. 84.—The Farmer shall, under the direction of the Governor, have supervision and charge of the farm and garden belonging to the Institution, and of the laborers and servants employed thereon from time to time; of all buildings and fences outside of the enclosure, all live stock and poultry, and all crops, produce, materials, vehicles, utensils, tools, &c., appertaining thereto, and shall devote his whole time and attention to the discharge of his duties.

Sec. 85.—He shall receive a stated salary for his services, which shall be in lieu of all fees, commissions, gratuities or perquisites, directly or indirectly, except that he shall be allowed the use of the cottage and garden plot allotted for the Farmer, with the privilege to purchase bread and coal at cost price from the Harbor as he may require for his own family.

Sec. 86.—He shall, with the approval of the Governor, be authorized to employ such number of laborers as may be necessary to perform the work of his department at the proper times, and shall keep a strict account, in the books to be furnished him for the purpose, of the time of service of each employee under him. The compensations of such persons shall not exceed the usual current rates to be fixed by the Governor.

SEC. 87.—He shall take care that the farm buildings, fences, vehicles, utensils and tools are kept in good condition, and, when requested by the Governor, shall assist him in making improvements and all such repairs, alterations and renewals of and to the buildings, grounds, fences, walks, roads, shrubbery, trees, &c., within the enclosure of the Institution, as may have been duly authorized by the Board of Trustees, either by the By-Laws or otherwise.

SEC. 88.—He shall have the oversight and direction of the vegetable garden, and of the foreman and laborers therein employed, taking care that sufficient ground is allotted to raise a full supply of all the ordinary vegetables needed for the Institution ; also that the planting, cultivating, gathering, and delivering to the Steward, or housing of all such vegetables, are duly and properly attended to.

SEC. 89.—He shall take care that the portions of the Farm appropriated for cultivation are planted in due season, with such crops as may be directed or approved by the Governor ; that the tending, gathering and securing of all crops are done in a proper manner, and at the right time.

SEC. 90.—He shall also see that the horses, cattle, swine and poultry are all duly cared for, and that all the pork, poultry, milk and eggs necessary for the use of the Institution, are produced upon the farm ; and in case of a short supply of either of these articles, the orders of the Physician for the Hospital shall be first provided for.

SEC. 91.—It shall be the duty of the Farmer to collect during the year, as far as may be practicable, a supply of fertilizing materials to maintain the land in proper condition, and in case of a short supply, to apply to the Governor for such additional quantity as may be needed.

SEC. 92.—He shall superintend the Cemetery, and take care that the same, with its fences and shrubbery, is kept in proper order and repair.

SEC. 93.—He shall make requisitions upon the Governor for all articles needed in his department, and proceed to examine and certify the invoices thereof as is provided in Section 11 of Art. III. He shall also prepare and certify pay-rolls of work done under his supervision, specifying names, number of days' labor and amount of wages due to each, which must be sent to the Governor for his approval.

SEC. 94.—He shall keep careful accounts of all produce delivered by him to the Steward, and receive credit for the same from the latter in a Pass Book kept for that purpose.

SEC. 95.—He shall, upon notice from the Governor or Steward, attend to the proper delivery of all supplies and materials landed at the Dock, or procured in the neighborhood, for the use of the Institution.

SEC. 96.—He shall make a quarterly report to the Governor, as required by Sec. 13 of Art. V., giving a statement of the work performed in his department during the preceding quarter.

SEC. 97.—The ENGINEER, under the direction of the Governor, shall have charge and supervision of all the engines, water-works, heating and cooking apparatus, gas-works, bath-rooms and water-closets, and of the machinery in the laundry, kitchen and elsewhere in and about the Institution; also of all repairs and renewals of the same. He shall also attend to all necessary repairs of the metallic roofs of buildings and other tin-work, the repairs of the iron fences and other iron-work, including the farm utensils and vehicles, and all plumbing work required about the premises, and shall devote the whole of his time to the discharge of his duties.

SEC. 98.—He shall receive a stated salary for his services, which shall be in lieu of all fees, commissions, gratuities or perquisites, directly or indirectly, except that he shall be allowed the use of the cottage allotted for his residence and garden plot.

SEC. 99.—He shall, with the approval of the Governor, be authorized to employ, when necessary, not exceeding two helpers, whose compensation shall be determined by the Executive Committee.

SEC. 100.—He shall make requisitions upon the Governor for all materials needed in his department, and shall examine and certify the invoices thereof, as provided in Section 11 of Art. III.

SEC. 101.—He shall keep careful accounts of all work done, and make a quarterly report to the Governor, as required by Sec. 13 of Art. V., giving a statement of the work performed in his department during the preceding quarter.

SEC. 102.—The MATRON shall, under the direction of the Governor, have charge of the laundry and the persons employed in it, and of all the work of making, washing, ironing and mending the clothes of the inmates, and the bedding and linen of the Institution; and shall devote her whole time to the performance of her duties. None but a single woman shall be eligible to this office.

SEC. 103.—She shall receive a stated salary, to be fixed by the Board of Trustees, together with the use of the furnished dwelling-house allotted for her residence, with lights, fuel and such provisions, groceries, vegetables and milk, from the stores of the Institution, as may be sufficient for herself and the women under her charge ; the quantities of each to be agreed upon from time to time with the Governor, subject to the approval of the Trustees, and to be served to her by the Steward.

SEC. 104.—She shall, with the approval of the Governor, be authorized to employ a cook and other persons necessary to perform the work in her department, whose compensations shall not exceed the usual rates, and be fixed by the Governor. Said women shall live in the apartments appropriated for their use in the Matron's house, and take their meals there, separate from the inmates and male servants. Unless otherwise expressly permitted by the matron, they shall always be in their rooms by nine o'clock at night.

SEC. 105.—She shall visit the rooms of the inmates, including those in the Hospital, at least once a week, see that the beds are kept clean and in good order, and report if they are not so to the Steward.

SEC. 106.—She shall take care that the clothing of the inmates is properly washed, ironed and mended, and that each person receives his own.

SEC. 107.—Articles of bedding required for the Hospital shall be furnished only on the requisition of the Physician, and shall be receipted for by the Nurse, who shall at the same time deliver to the Matron the soiled or worn-out pieces intended to be replaced thereby.

SEC. 108.—Inmates and servants shall not be allowed in the clothes-room or laundry. The Matron shall report to the Steward any violation of this rule.

SEC. 109.—On the death of any inmate the Matron shall receive from the Nurse attending him such clothes and bedding as may have been supplied by the Institution, and shall have them washed and repaired; the bedding to be retained in her care, and the clothes to be given to the Steward.

SEC. 110.—She shall from time to time take an inventory, in a book kept for that purpose, labeled "Inventory," of all beds, bedding, towels, table-cloths and other such articles belonging to the Institution, and furnish a copy thereof to the Governor, with a statement of the articles, if any, missing.

SEC. 111.—She shall keep an account in a book, labeled "Record Book," of all garments or articles received each week to be washed and repaired, with the names of the inmates to whom they belong, or rooms where used.

SEC. 112.—She shall also keep a careful account of all goods or materials received for making articles for the use of the Institution, comparing such materials with their invoices, and if found correct, the latter to be certified by her to the Governor, as provided by Section 11 of Article III.

SEC. 113.—She shall once a quarter, or oftener if required, prepare a list of the stock of materials on hand, either made up or not; of the number of beds, sheets, blankets and other articles of bedding in use and out of use, with remarks as to its condition &c., for the information of the Governor. She shall also, when necessary, make requisitions upon him for any materials or articles required in her department, as provided by Section 9 of Article V.

SEC. 114.—She shall employ a Seamstress, under the direction of the Governor, to assist her in making up and mending the clothing, bedding &c., and have supervision of the work to be performed by her.

SEC. 115.—She shall take care that all worn-out sheets, pillow-cases, towels, table-cloths and all linen or cotton garments of inmates, and other like articles, are collected and saved, to be disposed of as the Governor shall direct.

Sec. 116.—The Matron, in the general execution of her duties, upon which the health and comfort of the inmates so much depend, is enjoined to keep good order in her house, and take care that the women under her charge faithfully and honestly perform their appointed duties, and that their deportment is orderly, quiet and respectful. She must also take care that no waste, destruction or loss of property occur.

Sec. 117.—All subordinate officers and others whose duties are not herein defined shall be subject to and obey the orders of the respective Heads of Departments under whom they are employed, and shall perform such duties as may be prescribed by said Heads of Departments, with the approval of the Governor.

ARTICLE VI.

ALTERATIONS OF THE BY-LAWS.

The foregoing By-Laws, or any of them, may at any regular meeting of the Board of Trustees, by a two-thirds vote of not less than five members, be repealed, altered, or suspended, as they may determine.

ARTICLE VII.

OF LEASES AND TRANSFERS OF THE SAME.

1. Separate leases, signed by the President and Secretary, shall be given for each lot of ground belonging to this Trust.

2. The lessees or sub-lessees shall pay all expenses and charges for leases, transfers and acknowledgments of the same.

ARTICLE VIII.

GENERAL REGULATIONS.

SECTION 1.—*Qualifications required for Admission.*—The persons for whose maintenance and support the Asylum, or Marine Hospital, known as "The Sailors' Snug Harbor," was erected and established, are described in the will of its founder, and also in the Act of Incorporation, as "AGED, DECREPIT and WORN-OUT SAILORS."

Persons of this description only are eligible to admission as beneficiaries of the Institution.

SEC. 2.—No person shall hereafter be admitted to the privileges of the Institution, or allowed to continue as an inmate thereof:

NOTE.---The 4th and 5th clauses do not apply to the present inmates.

(1.) Who is afflicted with a contagious disease, the latter to be determined through an examination by, and a report from, the Resident Physician.

(2.) Who is possessed of adequate means of self-support, either by his own labor or from other sources.

(3.) Who cannot furnish satisfactory evidence of his having sailed for at least five years under the flag of the United States, either in the merchant or naval service.

(4.) Who does not present an application to the Board of Trustees in the form prescribed for such purpose, signed by the applicant, and verified by his oath, if required, as to the statements therein made; also accompanied by any testimonials or documentary proof of his eligibility for admission, according to the Rules of the Institution.

(5.) Who does not sign a copy of the following agreement:

I,   , having been received as an inmate of The Sailors' Snug Harbor, do hereby agree to abstain from all intoxicating liquors, and to readily and cheerfully perform such labor and service in and about the

Institution and Farm as may be required of me by the Governor, without expecting or claiming any reward or remuneration therefor; also to attend church at least once every Sunday in the Sailors' Snug Harbor Chapel, unless excused by the Governor; also to conduct myself in a quiet, orderly manner, and to strictly obey all the rules and regulations of the Institution.

And in consideration of being provided with a comfortable home, with food, clothing and medical attendance, and the other privileges afforded, I do hereby make over to the Institution all such beds, bedding, furniture or clothes as I may bring to it for my own use.

SEC. 3.---All persons who are now or may hereafter be admitted to the privileges of the Institution, are on a footing of entire equality, being entitled to the same privileges, and subject to the same duties and obligations. All misconduct or willful violation of the Rules may be punished by deprivation of said privileges, or by suspension or expulsion.

SEC. 4.—The present and future inmates of the Sailors' Snug Harbor shall be divided into three classes:

The First Class to embrace the most able-bodied men, whose duty it shall be to assist in outdoor work and carry coal.

The Second Class to embrace all those who are not enrolled in the First or Third Class.

Their duty shall be to keep the buildings and walks clean, and assist in all indoor work.

The Third Class to embrace all those who, through physical disability, are excused by the Resident Physician from all labor.

SEC. 5.—*General Rules.*—The rising bell will be rung at such hour in the morning as the Governor may direct. The inmates shall at once rise, make their beds, tidy their rooms and persons, and at the ringing of the call-bell assemble for breakfast. They shall occupy the seats at table allotted or their use.

SEC. 6.—No inmate shall take his seat at table with unwashed face and hands, or in an uncleanly condition.

SEC. 7.—A proper person shall, by request of the Governor, ask a blessing at every meal. No inmate shall commence eating at table before a blessing shall have been asked.

SEC. 8.—Inmates are strictly forbidden to take any food from the dining halls, or to indulge in contention or boisterous and disorderly conversation at the table, and are earnestly enjoined to demean themselves in a decorous and becoming manner.

SEC. 9.—The general charge of the dining-rooms, halls, kitchen, bakery and dormitory shall, under the Governor, belong to the Steward, who shall be assisted in the performance of his duties by suitable persons among the inmates, to be approved by the Governor.

SEC. 10.—The setting of the tables, and the bringing in and removal of the dishes, shall be directed by the assistants; and it shall be the duty of every inmate to co-operate with them in an obliging manner, and to do all in his power to preserve order and regularity.

SEC. 11.—Inmates shall, under direction of the Steward, sweep daily the hall floors, wash the lower hall floors weekly, and keep clean the steps, areas, walks and grounds around the buildings. All will be expected to co-operate in keeping the buildings and grounds in perfect order.

SEC. 12.—Inmates who may be addicted to the use of tobacco and snuff will, under proper regulations, be furnished with a moderate supply of those articles; but no smoking shall be allowed in the halls or lodging-rooms, nor in any other part of the buildings except such as may be appropriated for that use by the Governor, and all spitting in and about the buildings is strictly forbidden.

SEC. 13.—Any inmate who may leave the premises while under "Taboo," or who shall assault any officer or inmate, or sell or otherwise dispose of clothing or other property furnished by or belonging to the Sailors' Snug Harbor, or who may bring any intoxicating liquor into the Institution,

Shall be *expelled.*

SEC. 14.—The use of intoxicating liquors, except when prescribed by a physician, is positively forbidden, and any inmate who shall be found guilty of drunkenness, shall, during a specified period, be deprived of the privileges of going outside the enclosure, and be otherwise punished, at the discretion of the Governor. In case of persistent violation of this rule, the inmate so offending shall be suspended by the Governor, and the case immediately reported to the Executive Committee.

SEC. 15.—Clothing of such style as shall be decided on by the Trustees, will be furnished to all inmates, and kept in repair; but no article shall be thus supplied without a written order from the Governor, and the delivery to the Steward of the old garment or article which the new one is to replace.

SEC. 16.—No inmate shall, without permission from the Governor, wear the clothing furnished by and belonging to the Institution while on leave of absence, neither shall he destroy, sell, exchange or otherwise dispose of any such clothing or other property of the Institution.

SEC. 17.—A condition of idleness and inactivity being always detrimental to health, all inmates shall be under obligation to perform such labor and service in and about the buildings, grounds and farm as may be required of them by the Governor. Any one claiming exemption from this regulation, by reason of disability, will be required to produce the Resident Physician's certificate of the fact, otherwise he will not be excused; and in case of refusal to comply he will be "Tabooed;" his tobacco will be stopped; he will be denied the use of the Library and Reading-room, and forbidden to do any work by which he can earn money.

SEC. 18.—Inmates are forbidden to work for persons outside of the Institution, without permission of the Governor : any one breaking this rule will be liable to be expelled.

SEC. 19.—A suitable room having been appropriated and furnished for holding daily religious exercises, the Chaplain will be in attendance both morning and evening to conduct the same, and all persons connected with the Institution are earnestly and most affectionately requested to avail themselves as often as may be practicable of this provision for their benefit.

SEC. 20.—All inmates will be allowed the privileges of the Library and Reading-room, under such regulations as are necessary to maintain good order in the rooms and preserve the books and papers from injury.

SEC. 21.—The hour for closing and locking the gates of the Institution throughout the year shall be 9 o'clock P. M., at which hour all inmates and servants must be within.

SEC. 22.—No light shall be allowed in any of the buildings after 9 o'clock in the evening, excepting the night-lamps in the halls and in the rooms of the sick, and it shall be the duty of the Steward to see that all other lights are extinguished.

SEC. 23.—*Leave of absence* may be granted by the Governor to any inmate in good standing, by written permit, which shall state the duration of such leave; and no inmate shall at any time be absent without such permission, under penalty of having his name stricken from the roll of beneficiaries. Inmates returning from leave shall immediately report in person to the Governor.

SEC. 24.—*All parcels and packages* brought to the Institution, by visitors or others, must be deposited with the lodge-keepers, who will return them when the owner leaves. If intended for any of the officers, such parcels will be delivered as addressed. If designed for any inmate or servant, such parcels shall be delivered by the lodge-keeper to the Steward, who shall cause the same to be opened in the presence of the person to whom it is addressed; and if any intoxicating liquor or other contraband article shall be found therein, the same shall be withheld and reported to the Governor. No inmate shall be allowed to take anything outside the gates without a written permit from the Governor or Steward; and it shall be the duty of the lodge-keepers to detain all parcels or articles for which proper permits are not produced, and report the same to the Governor. Pedlers are in no case to be allowed upon the premises. The lodge-keepers have authority to search any inmate who offers to pass in or out of the gate. Inmates must use the centre gate only, and are strictly prohibited from passing in or out of the West gate, Governor's gate, or Doctor's gate.

SEC. 25.—Work of all kinds is strictly prohibited on the Sabbath, unless expressly ordered by the Governor. All inmates who are not in church will be required to remain quietly in their own rooms during the hours of Divine service.

SEC. 26.—Each inmate will be furnished with his number stamped on metal; said number must be tied on his bundle of clothes when taken to the wash-house, and will be returned to him with his clean clothes.

Sec. 27.—Inmates in good standing who faithfully perform the duties assigned to them will, by the permission of the Governor, be allowed to make baskets or mats, or do other work by which they can earn money for their own use, provided that they readily and cheerfully put aside said work to obey any orders they may receive from the Governor or Steward.

Sec. 28.—It is hereby made the duty of every one connected with the Institution to report to the Governor any instance within his knowledge of the willful waste or destruction of property, or any depredations thereon, as well as any violations of the Rules and Regulations of the Institution.

www.ingramcontent.com/pod-product-compliance
Lightning Source LLC
Chambersburg PA
CBHW031453270326
41930CB00007B/984